THE INVISIBLE HOLOCAUST

The Story of Ruth Ravina

MARLEN GABRIEL

Editor

DANIEL GABRIEL

VALLENTINE MITCHELL

LONDON • CHICAGO

First published in 2023 by Vallentine Mitchell

Catalyst House,
720 Centennial Court,
Centennial Park, Elstree WD6 3SY, UK

814 N. Franklin Street,
Chicago, Illinois,
60610 USA

www.vmbooks.com

British Library Cataloguing in Publication Data:
An entry can be found on request

ISBN 978 1 80371 037 2 (paper)
ISBN 978 1 80371 038 9 (ebook)

Library of Congress Cataloging in Publication Data:
An entry can be found on request

Contents

Acknowledgements

I want to thank Mark Ravina who encouraged me and helped me with many details – such as stories about his grandmother Pola, which she told him when he visited her while a student at Columbia University. I was struck by his eagerness to learn more about the fate of his mother, and by his showing great appreciation for my work on the book. In the end, he convinced me to incorporate my own childhood war experiences into those of his mother to give the work a different dimension.

I also thank Mel Rosenthal, who provided important assistance on questions relating to Hebrew and Yiddish, and to Jewish customs; and Barbara Wind for introducing me to Ruth and for her encouragement of the work. Thanks to Danuta Metz for her help with Polish; and Synnöve Trier-Engelman for her comments on the book, particularly about my own thoughts and reflections on Ruth's story. I also want to thank Sebastian Uhlmann for his artistic and technical assistance; and finally, Axel Haase for his valuable professional advice.

Prologue

'My cousin Rose, Ruczka as we called her, told me what I'm now relating to you,' Ruth said. 'It was a long time ago that she told me this story – sometime after we had landed in New York.'

'It was on the second day of Passover in the year 1937 in Poland,' cousin Rose began. 'Aunt Pola was worried about giving birth in Kozienice, though at that time, it was a custom to give birth at home. Two of her sisters-in-law had died at home in childbirth.

Therefore, Aunt Pola arranged to give birth in Warsaw in a hospital with a doctor. She came some weeks before to Warsaw to stay with her sister Tzipora.

That year I, my husband, and all the other relatives from Warsaw and its surroundings had come to commemorate Passover together with Aunt Pola and Uncle Motek, at the apartment of Aunt Tzipora, Uncle Israel, and Sarah.

Uncle Israel as our host led the *Seder*. After breaking the matzo bread – the bread of our affliction – with the youngest child, his daughter Sarah, asking the four questions, he began to tell the story of Passover.

As he was just reading about Moses taking his people out of Egypt and out of slavery, suddenly Aunt Pola, who was already in labor, became increasingly nervous. She was gliding back and forth on the bench at the table, and then cried out: 'I can't stand it anymore! I have to go!'

She forgot about the commemoration and the *Seder* to follow, about the good food, which she had helped her sister Tzipora prepare days before, waiting in the kitchen to be shared: *gefilte fish*; chicken broth with *kneydlach* made from the best matzo meal; and a fattened-up goose with potatoes and plenty of vegetables.

We all forgot about the commemoration and the delicious food and the wine.

First Aunt Pola and Uncle Motek rushed out of the apartment, then I, followed by my husband, and Sarah and all the other relatives. Like a flock of birds, we all hurried through the snow-covered streets of Warsaw to the hospital to witness the birth of little Ruth.'

1

Meeting Ruth

On a late September day, I took the train from New York Penn Station to New Jersey for my first meeting with Ruth to interview her. Soon the train left and after a while it emerged out of the tunnel under the streets of New York.

I was thinking of Ruth; how I had met her at the *Seder* of a mutual friend before I was going to leave for the summer in Germany; and how I took a liking to her, sitting next to her and listening to her talk about her childhood in Poland; and how I had called her and told her that I wanted to tell her story.

Of course, I realized how difficult it would be for her to tell her story to someone outside the circle of her family and friends, particularly to a German. And I remembered how Ruth told me that she had tried to write her memories down, but each time fell into a depression. But after the death of her husband, nevertheless, she told her story in lectures at public schools, civic centers, synagogues, and churches, mainly to young people.

I wondered how in this form of public presentation she was able to overcome the difficulties of her Holocaust past when the possibility of writing about it overwhelmed her. Did Ruth simply need someone who would listen to her and was it now the right time?

Later, when I tried to record Ruth's words, which at times would send shivers down my spine or take my breath away, when Ruth was describing her will to survive in the camps in Poland under German military command, what did I myself feel?

I had told Ruth that I was not much younger than her, that I was born at the beginning of the war; that my mother with my two older brothers and I fled the bombing of Hamburg, my hometown; and that we were evacuated to the eastern part of Germany during and after the war.

'There are going to be parallels in our childhood war experiences,' Ruth told me. 'You lived your childhood during the war in Germany, and I, the Jewish child, lived in the ghetto, and later was hidden in three forced labor camps in Poland.'

Later, as I was interviewing Ruth I learned about the child with the curly hair, the brave little girl on her long path of suffering. Reflections on her story would in turn provoke memories of my own childhood during the war.

Are we adults really capable of comprehending a child's suffering during war? I asked myself.

A few days after I had called Ruth she called me back. 'Yes,' she said, 'I want you to tell my story.'

As I was looking forward to seeing Ruth again the train was going through a desolate landscape, past abandoned houses without windows and with sunken-in rooftops, industrial areas surrounded by high wire fences stretching along waterways. Wild birds flew up from tiny islands and a big haggard dog sat motionless in a lonely wasteland.

Soon we stopped in Newark with its high rises and old water towers. Then we passed endless rows of wooden houses with their gardens in tree-lined streets. We were coming through more prosperous communities now; and as the train pulled into the station of Watchung Avenue, named after the Indian tribe that lived in this area when the early settlers came, I saw Ruth waiting for me on the platform.

She had come in her car. We drove up to her house. Proudly she told me that it had been built during the Depression in the early thirties.

'I lived in this house with my husband Oscar and our two sons. Now it's much too big for me. But I don't really want to move to another place,' she said as she turned the key in the door. 'I never had a real home. I was about three and a half when we went into the ghetto.'

After Ruth had shown me her house full of memories of her husband, a former violinist at the New York Philharmonic – his violins, his piano, the last music he played before his death, still on a music stand – we settled into the kitchen. She had prepared lunch for us, and soon we started to talk about her past.

'Why don't you just start with your first memory?' I suggested.

'Before I start to tell you my story,' Ruth said, 'you need to know, that almost my entire family perished in the Holocaust. I was only a small child when the killing of my very large family happened.

Many of my memories come from my mother and my cousin Sarah, who both survived the war with me, and also from Ruczka, my oldest surviving cousin later in New York.

My own memories probably became tainted or were even destroyed by the traumatic experiences I went through during these war years. Of course,

I must have suppressed a lot or confused certain events. My memory, particularly when it comes to my family, lacks discipline and shows the chaos I lived in.

Bear with me during my effort to remember my family members who are long dead, and whom I mostly never met. Sometimes my search may not follow a chronological order. Again, bear with me, and let's do this together.'

I realized in hindsight that Ruth needed to share her family's story at great length. During our interviews she was experiencing her past as a great pain both deep and prolonged.

2

Ruth's Family and Kozienice

'The first event I remember very clearly was my second birthday,' Ruth began. 'I was told that my big birthday present was coming: my paternal Grandmother Toba, whom I had never met.

She finally made a trip from her hometown Przemysl to visit me in Kozienice, a small town in central Poland south of Warsaw. She kept putting that trip off because she was hoping that current rumors about the threat of war would settle down. No matter whom you were talking to the subject of war kept coming up.

Toba's husband, my Grandpa Israel, was in a wheelchair. He was an invalid from World War I. Grandma Toba was determined to meet at least one of her grandchildren. The other grandchild was living in Argentina. She probably was resigned to the fact that she never would meet her other grandchild.

Grandma Toba's other daughter was Scheindl, the only child of theirs who also lived in Przemysl. Scheindl was by that time newly married. She finally persuaded her husband to move in with her parents for a month, so Toba could go to see Ruth.

Later Aunt Scheindl had two babies in the ghetto. There is only one photo taken in the ghetto – Scheindl with her mother, my Grandma Toba. I looked very much like Aunt Scheindl with my thick curly hair.

Toba was coming for the summer, the summer of 1939. And it was the most exciting thing!' Ruth laughed. 'I was used to an old grandma, my mother's mother, Grandma Miriam. That grandma was wearing long dresses and all. We lived in an apartment in my grandparents' house. Grandma Miriam and Grandpa Leib had a very large house.

Then Grandma Toba arrived: a young grandma, who was wearing high heels. She was only in her fifties. She would chase me and run with me.

My parents had put her bed next to my crib. In the morning when I woke up she whispered: 'Sh, be quiet.'

She took me out of the crib. She didn't want my mom and dad to wake up. And then we played. My favorite thing was to walk in her shoes with the high heels. She put on her wig because she was an Orthodox woman.

Then we ran around our apartment, through the kitchen and back, and she pretended to catch me.

Those were really the first memories I have,' Ruth said. 'Before that time, it's all very vague. Perhaps still having breakfast with my mom, and then the nanny came in because mom had to open the shop at ten. I also remember having breakfast with mom, and watching her comb her hair. She had long hair and she made braids, put them up this way and also that way.' Ruth showed me.

Ruth, Pola, father Motek, and Grandmother Toba 1939

'I think you have those also in Germany, right? Anyway, I'm having a lovely time with Grandma Toba and we go to the lake, we do all kinds of fun things. But then suddenly, grandma went back to Przemysl. The Germans were on the march already towards Poland.

Grandmother Toba had four children. My father was the oldest. She also had two daughters: Sarah, who had moved to Argentina with her husband already before the war, and Scheindl. She also had a younger son I never met.

That son, my mom told me later, was twenty-eight at the beginning of the war. His name was Wolf. He was an officer in the Polish army. He was captured. There was one letter from him. He wrote he was very worried because nobody knew he was a Jew. But if they had found out there would have been trouble.

It was 1939! That was sometime in October.

Next thing we heard was from Argentina. Grandma Toba had informed her daughter Sarah in Argentina that her brother Wolf had come home. And Aunt Sarah had written us.

You could get letters more easily from a foreign country,' Ruth explained. 'You couldn't get letters locally. The whole postal service got messed up, like the whole country did.

We got a letter from Aunt Sarah saying that Wolf was at home. We found out that he had escaped from a German prisoner of war camp before being discovered as a Jew. He swam the San, Poland's second largest river, came home, just as they were forming the ghetto in Przemysl.

He went from the frying pan into the fire or whatever you want to call it.'

'Do you know anything about the Przemysl ghetto?'

'No, I don't.'

'Do you know what happened to Wolf?'

'He probably died in some forced labor camp. Aunt Scheindl, her husband, and their two babies also perished, and, of course, Toba and Israel Kalb, because nobody knew anything from that branch of the family again.'

Ruth fell silent, then after a while she continued.

'I remember that, but not much more. But I remember going to the courtyard of my grandparents' house. There were flowers and an herb garden. At the very end of the court there was my father's shop.

My mother and her brother Maier also owned a shop. That was in town next to the pub. It was in the most Christian part of town. They rented the property from the owner of a pub.

Every now and then I would run over the courtyard to my father's shop. I remember the smell of sawdust. I didn't quite understand what my dad

Scheindl and Toba in the Ghetto in Przemysl 1940

was doing. I only saw that he always had a flat pencil in his hand, and he would draw on the wood with that pencil.

He would say: 'You cut it out,' or 'you sand it.' My father had five workmen and six apprentices.

My mother told me later that he only made custom furniture. If you wanted something special he would design it for you. Or if you had lost some piece of furniture because of a fire, you would bring a photograph, and he would make the exact same thing. His customers were more like the gentry. Because it was all custom made.

Ah, he was teaching very fine cabinet making. That's what he had learned in Austria,' Ruth proudly told me.

'And he spoke German?'

'Yes, his whole family did. And Polish and Yiddish. Yiddish was really the common language. My Grandma Toba spoke to Grandma Miriam in Yiddish, because she was raised in German, and Grandma Miriam was raised in Polish. Yiddish could bring Jews from all the sections together.

We got mail from Grandma Toba until well into the war, because Toba, of course, wrote in German to her son. The Germans censored the letters, blackened out words or passages, but my father could somehow figure out the rest. Most of the people in the ghettos wrote in Yiddish or Polish. So that mail didn't get through.

My father had an unusual situation. He might have been the only Jew in Poland who was a *Meister,* a master craftsman, because he had gotten his education in Austria. His father, Israel Kalb, whom I never met, was an invalid, as I told you. He had been an officer in the Austro-Hungarian army. He got wounded in World War I.

Therefore, his sons were entitled to certain educational privileges. My father went to school in Vienna, I believe, but I'm not sure. I just know he had an Austrian license. And that what had been Austria is now Poland.

You couldn't have the license in Poland because the guilds were Catholic. A Jew could not belong to a Catholic guild.'

'What privileges did your father have?'

'A *Meister's* certificate gave him permission to teach and train workers.'

'They didn't have to be Jewish?'

'They didn't have to be Jewish. They could have been Jewish, Christian, or anything. He trained them until they became journeymen. Then they could go and work for anybody else. Yes, that was a privilege he had, which Jews in Poland didn't have. They could be workers, but they did not have the license to train others, which was a great privilege.

To me it was very important that he had some Christian apprentices, because one of them was Maciek. He became a great help to me when I needed help desperately.'

Ruth had a bunch of old pictures spread out on the kitchen table. She pointed at one of them. 'This is Aunt Sarah from Argentina. I think it was in 1964, because I took her to the World's Fair in Queens. She came to visit us in New York. She said that she wasn't going to miss the only relative she has left.'

'And that's you.' I pointed at a little girl with thick curly hair. Her mother is holding her in her arms. Next to Ruth's mother there is also Grandma Toba and her son Motek.

'Yes, that's me. It was during the summer when Grandma Toba visited,' Ruth explained. And then she picked up a newer picture of her son Mark.

'He was just born,' Ruth said with great pride in her voice. 'My first child had just been born.

Aunt Sarah's mother Toba was blond. My cousin Sarah was blond and blue-eyed too. My son Mark was also born blue-eyed and blond.'

'Aunt Sarah is your Grandmother Toba's daughter?'

'Yes. Grandma Toba had two daughters. That's her other daughter.' Ruth pointed at another picture.

'This was already taken in the ghetto of Przemysl. It's a year later. This is my Aunt Scheindl, I already told you about. I can't read the small print under the picture,' Ruth complained.

'It says,' I read to her, 'Ruth's Grandmother Toba Kalb with her youngest daughter.'

'I never knew Aunt Scheindl,' Ruth said. 'I don't know anything about her, except they got married and had two little boys. All of them were in the ghetto of Przemysl. Nobody survived, I also already told you.'

Ruth fell silent for a while. Then she went on remembering more about her once very large family.

'Now let me tell you how my parents met. My mother met my father in Przemysl. Uncle Daniel, my mother's middle brother, had asked whether Pola, my mother, who was then sixteen years old, could help in their shop because his wife had a difficult pregnancy. They had a children's clothing shop and it was difficult for him to manage alone.

After the first stay in Przemysl, only a day's train ride from Kozienice, my mother kept finding reasons to visit her brother Daniel every summer. She had fallen in love with this young man Motek, who later became my father.

As the years went by Uncle Daniel could no longer think of excuses to ask for Pola, why she should be coming for the summer to spend with his family. So, his sister Tzeytel took over. Both were in on the secret that Pola and Grandma Toba's son Motek were romantically involved.

Aunt Tzeytel, Pola's oldest sister, had by then five children. They were well off, owned a tannery in a town not far from Przemysl. 'We have five children,' she wrote to my grandparents, 'and it would be very nice if Pola could come and spend the summer with them.'

I am sure my grandparents must have wondered why Pola should spend all these summers out there.

After five years, Pola finally told her parents. And since everyone knew about the romance and agreed that they were a good fit, her parents gave in. They, of course, were accustomed to choose husbands for their daughters, according to tradition.

But that was not for Pola, my mother. She had her own will, and wanted to choose herself the man she loved.

Oh, my mother told me, that when her oldest sister Tzeytel was to be married, her mother, Grandma Miriam, sewed a fancy pink dress for her two-year-old daughter. But Pola absolutely wanted a white dress like the bride was going to wear. She threw a tantrum. She wanted a white dress like the bride.

The next thing my mother became aware of was that she was sleeping in her pink dress on her parents' big bed, and when she woke up the wedding was over.

These are just morsels I remember my mother telling me,' Ruth sighed. 'I wish I knew more about my large, lively family.

But I still remember hearing that Grandma Toba was very worried that her son Motek would marry a girl from out of town, because she counted on his income to help the family. Her husband, Israel Kalb, had only a tiny pension from being an officer in World War I.

My mother's father, Grandpa Leib, who owned land he rented out, built a carpentry shop with living space for apprentices for his future son-in-law, according to my father's specifications. Grandpa felt that Motek had a profession, that things were done by order and that they were delivered. This way he could work in his profession in Kozienice and send money to help his family in Przemysl.

And Pola, their youngest child, felt she had to take care of her parents in Kozienice, because tradition calls for the youngest to take care of the old parents.'

At our next interview Ruth added more detail about her grandparents: 'We were living in my grandparents' house, with my Grandma Miriam and Grandpa Leib. Our windows faced the front and there was grandpa's hardware store, a leather shop, and another store. Next to grandpa's store was our apartment.

We had an entrance from the front street and from the side street. In the kitchen there was a connecting door to a hallway leading to my grandparents' apartment, from which we could get to the courtyard.

Every tenant that my grandfather had, had a store in the front, and they lived in the back. They used the back entrance to their home. They used the pump in the courtyard. It belonged to my grandparents. But it was a communal courtyard for everybody.

My father's shop was at the furthest end of the courtyard. On one side there were something like sheds. There my father kept the dry wood, the lumber that he needed.

The front street was a major street. I think that it was called Radomska Street. The side street later on became a ghetto street. We were Number 16 on that street called Lubelska Street. I am sure of that.

Now, let me tell you about my cousin Sarah, with whom I spent the entire war,' Ruth suggested. 'My mother's sister, Tzipora Luksenburg, was designing clothes and her husband, Israel Lichtenstein, was a sculptor. They lived in Warsaw.' Ruth pointed at another picture. 'This is my cousin Sarah, their only child.

My grandparents Miriam and Leib had a large house in the Lake Country of Poland. All grandchildren kept popping in for a few weeks' vacation in the summer. They rented a shed near the lake, which was in walking distance from the house.

I remember sitting in my stroller being rolled down to the lake. In the shed were deck chairs, a folding table, dishes, spoons, and forks. Grandma would bring enough food to spend an entire day by the lake. When everyone had finished eating she would wash the dishes in the lake.

The summers with all the grandchildren visiting – that was the joy of my grandparents' life. Life before the war.

Now, since Sarah lived in a big crowded city her mother would always bring her as soon as school was out. She would stay over the whole summer. And either her mother or her father would come at the end of summer and take her back.

During the war years, well already in 1939, I guess it was decided that Sarah shouldn't go back, because in the big cities there was immediately a shortage of food. So, Sarah stayed. Sarah never saw her parents again.'

'What happened? What happened to Sarah's parents?'

'She stayed with us. Her parents died in the Warsaw Ghetto at some point. We don't know when.

The Warsaw Ghetto was totally annihilated and destroyed. Not like smaller ghettos where people had a chance to hide with peasants occasionally or go into the forest or anything like that.

Sarah became my mother's second child,' Ruth said.

'And she became like a sister to you?'

'Yes, we were like sisters. Basically, we grew up as sisters. Even after the war when we had meager residences, we never had one big enough that Sarah and I had a separate bed.

We were sleeping – in Yiddish you'd say: *Tzu kop un tzu fis.* We were sleeping head to toe in the same bed. Well, we were kicking each other half the night, most of the time lovingly.' Remembering that scene Ruth gave a big laugh.

'Sarah was later adopted, and she left before me to the United States. That was because of my cousin Rose. We called her Ruczka.

I hope I won't confuse you with my large family. But bear with me. Now we'll have to go to the end of my ordeal, because after the war Ruczka did everything possible to get us over to America.

My mother's older brother Yechel lived near Warsaw. He had two children, Daniel and Rose. Daniel died in the Przemysl ghetto with his wife and two children. Rose, that's Ruczka, survived because already in the summer of 1939 Ruczka and her first husband left Poland.

Her husband was involved with the Jewish labor movement. He was a union organizer. They felt it wasn't safe for him to stay.

At that time an American union leader, David Dubinski, president of the Ladies' Garment Workers' Union, was trying to rescue as many Jewish labor leaders as possible. He managed through political connections to designate a certain number of visas for Jewish labor leaders from Poland to come to the United States.

Ruczka's husband obtained a visa from the United States. They were looking for a route to get out of Poland. She told me later in New York that they first went to Lithuania, which was sovereign at that time, where they applied at the consulate in Kaunas for a transit visa to Japan. They crossed Russia on the Trans-Siberian Railroad to Vladivostok, and from there took a boat to Japan.

After some short but nerve-racking time waiting for a ship, they finally were on their way to the United States, to Seattle; and from there they took a train to New York.

Finally, they landed in New York. There Ruczka's husband fell ill and died, because he had kidney failure while they were travelling. They had no medical care during their travels.'

'After the war Ruczka brought Sarah to the United States,' you told me.

'Yes. Ruczka was now a widow and all Jewish immigrants from Poland were sort of staying cliquish together. She had been a Red Cross nurse in Poland, so she was now working for the Visiting Nurse Service of New York. She had a pretty well-paying job. After the war she was looking for family and she wrote to everywhere and everyone.

Ruczka was one of the bigger kids who used to come every summer to my grandparents' house too. She was only two years younger than my mother. For me they were sort of aunt and cousin, because of all the children in between.'

While Ruth was looking through the photographs she always kept on the table, she again pointed to one.

'The last summer Ruczka came,' she explained, 'she came to say good-bye. Later when she was dying in New York – she was almost a hundred years old – she told me how she always remembered taking the train from Warsaw to Kozienice, and that she never missed a visit to her grandparents' house for the summer.

Anyway, Ruczka was a widow now and she was in touch with all the Jewish immigrants in New York,' Ruth continued. 'She met a gentleman from Krakow who couldn't find his wife and daughter. They were sort of seeing each other. Finally, he found his son who was in his late teens already, nineteen, in a boys' home in Italy.

'What if we marry?' he asked Ruczka. 'Then I'll bring my son here.'

'Of course, you will,' my cousin said.

They brought his son and while he was working on this, it occurred to Ruczka they should also have Sarah come.

'What if we adopt Sarah? Then we can bring Sarah too.' And that's what they did.'

When we met again, Ruth suggested that we return to Kozienice to continue the story about the other side of her family.

'We'll need some explanation here for you. Again, my father was the first child of Grandma Toba, Sarah the second, then the other sister Scheindl, and then came Wolf. She had four children.'

'That's Grandma Toba, with the high heels?'

'Yes, she wore high heels. Not too Orthodox. Well, she was a modern Orthodox and just wore a wig. But not like my maternal grandma Miriam. Grandma Miriam had nine children, my mother being the youngest.

My mother's father is Leib Luksenburg. He was the youngest of ten children. Leib Luksenburg, my grandfather. In Yiddish *leib* means lion. That family was big.

Before the war Grandpa Leib had a hardware store. His major customers had been blacksmiths. But because of modernization – there were now buses and trains running, and people arriving at the train station would no longer take a carriage drawn by horses – his business was slowing down.

But he stubbornly wanted to keep the store going because it was still worthwhile on Wednesdays, the market day. He could sell blacksmiths' supplies since the country folk were depending on the items he kept in stock. At that time peasants were still plowing their fields with horses. During the rest of the week there was a bell in the kitchen that would ring if a blacksmith needed supplies.

That my Grandpa Leib kept the shop running was very helpful for us, once the Germans moved in,' Ruth explained.

'Your father's business was in the backyard, right? Where was your grandfather's store?'

'My grandfather had the front store on one of the main streets. I believe the street was called Radomska Street, as I already mentioned. It was – just think of a square block.'

Ruth drew for me a picture of her grandparents' property in my notebook. Now I was able to visualize her grandparents' house where Ruth spent the days of her early childhood, and where all her cousins were coming for the summer.

'Next to grandfather's store were two other stores. In the back of that square there was my father's shop,' she added.

'Your mother also had a store, you said.'

'Yes, my mother together with her brother Maier had a store in the other part of town, in a very stylish Polish part of town. Kozienice is a small town. It was all in walking distance. Maybe it was four blocks away.

Oh, I must tell you how that shop came into being,' Ruth said laughing. 'Well, that's what my mother told me. Her brother Maier, who had lost his wife and child in childbirth, had come back to stay with his parents in Kozienice.

After the mourning period he decided to leave for Warsaw to study. My grandparents, of course, wanted to help him. He left to study in Warsaw staying with his oldest sister Tzipora. His parents wanted him to become a rabbi, of course. But he came back with a degree in electrical engineering.

He convinced his sister Pola, my mother, to open an electric supply shop in Kozienice. Pola who thought highly of her brother, this time believed him to be absolutely crazy, because only a third of Kozienice had electricity at that time. It was in the first quarter of the twentieth century!' Ruth cried. 'Imagine.

Uncle Maier however insisted: 'With your head for business and my knowledge of electricity, it's going to work. I'll have the rest of town electrified.' Which he did. He hired people and soon electrified the entire town.

'Everyone will want to have a radio,' he convinced his sister. 'You'll see. Everyone will want to listen to the news.'

And they opened their shop, an electric supply shop. The radios were just jumping off the shelves,' Ruth exclaimed. 'And they also sold plenty of electric irons. Every woman wanted to have her own electric iron.

Kozienice means many things. It literally means goat town – there were many goats in the area and they contributed to the town's economic life,' Ruth explained to me. 'There were tanneries. Near Radom Grandpa Leib's sister's family had a tannery. They were quite well off.

The whole region, the whole county, goats were essential: for milk, cheese, leather. That was the basic farming, but of course, they would grow vegetables, sugar beets, and potatoes. But what they did for sale were the goats.'

'On Wednesday it was market day, you told me.'

'Yes, because it was people from villages and from the countryside who came. That was a big day. You could shop for food, you could shop for handicraft, shoes, anything.'

'It must have been a lot of fun for you with all the people coming and going, and all the fancy things!'

Ruth nodded, smiling.

'And your father's shop was also open all day on market day?'

'No, my father's shop wasn't, because his shop wasn't really open to the public. He only made custom furniture. His shop was in the back of grandpa's property.

Previously, Leib's wife, Grandma Miriam . . . that family for many generations was actually living way out in the country, because Grandma Miriam's father and her grandfather, and maybe generations before, had all been the managers of Polish counts who preferred to live in Vienna. They ran their estate.

The Goldberg family had five daughters, my Grandmother Miriam being the middle one. Since the count, at the time, wanted them to have their families close he was offering them positions on the estate. One son-in-law ran the mill, another ran the lumberyard, because there was a lot of lumber.

My Grandfather Leib was running the brewery. He didn't mind, but because he was a city boy he was bored. He had been a city boy in a merchant family and he hated the country.

Grandma Miriam's parents didn't want my grandma to be far away. 'I'll set your husband up in any business in the market town of Kozienice,' her father decided, 'because I can come by horse and carriage in an hour or so.'

My mother told me, when she was a little girl, a very little girl, she remembered traveling by horse and carriage, with the count's insignia on the doors and with four white horses. She was going to visit grandpa or coming back from visiting grandpa.

And the one thing she particularly remembered, was when the count's standard, the flag, wasn't up the peasants in the field would continue working. If the count were in the carriage the standard would be up. Then the peasants would have to kneel down next to the crops. My mother thought that was an odd thing because it was the same carriage.

These were some of the stories I heard my mother telling me during those long cold nights in the camps. My mother always told me stories in the camps, family stories mostly, to keep me both informed and entertained during those horrible years. She wanted to calm me when I was hungry and cold, and wanted to teach me all about my family.

'Those stories are very important,' she would say to me. 'If you survive you will know your family. You will know who you are and where you come from.'

For her it was a sort of survival manual.

But let's go back to Grandma Miriam. She was very comfortable in Polish, both in language and custom, because she lived among Polish people.'

'Do you have a picture of her?'

'No, they were so religious they wouldn't take pictures,' Ruth explained. 'There are none. They were too religious for that. I actually don't remember ever seeing grandma's hair. It had always been covered. Grandpa had a beautiful long white beard. That's how I remember him. In his youth he was a redhead.

My parents came from two different worlds. Neither of them was very religious. They each celebrated the holidays only to please their families. My mother told me that they were culturally very Jewish but religiously very liberal. Their belief was that people could change the world but God couldn't.'

Ruth wanted to return to her thoughts about her family before the ghetto, when we next met. 'My mother grew up Orthodox, but by the time she was twelve she started thinking of the world for herself.

Now, the shoemakers' boys, and there were a lot of shoemakers in my town, mostly were working for the Bata Shoe Factory in Czechoslovakia. They were having the soft leather tops made in this area where the leather was coming from. It was a cottage industry and it was paid by the piece. Soft like glove leather, the very fine leather. Because of the numerous goats our town was in the leather and dairy industries.

One day my mother became aware, that Polish young men were paid better than the Jewish young men. And she figured it out because there was a piece of paper they had to sign. The Jewish young men were sent to *cheder,* which means Hebrew School. They could read and write Hebrew. But they couldn't read the contract. They signed with an 'X' and they paid them whatever they wanted to pay.

At the age of twelve, my mother took it upon herself to change this. If they can read the contract they will get better pay, she thought. And instead of going to synagogue on Saturdays she taught the young shoemakers how to read Polish, because Hebrew didn't do them any good. They could just read the prayer book.

She was their teacher. Her father was very upset about this. 'A young girl from a good middle-class family hanging out with shoemakers ten years older than her! This is unconscionable! This is not acceptable!' he exclaimed.

'Papa, I need to teach them how to read!' she contradicted him. And she did.'

'That's wonderful, Ruth!'

'But it caused my mother to get several spankings. Her father hit her with a cane, because someone came who said she was writing on a Sabbath. He saw it because the French doors were open. But she wasn't. She was using a pointer. But she got beaten up because writing on a Sabbath is a sin when you're Orthodox.

It caused my mother a lot of pain,' Ruth added. 'But she became a beloved figure in our town. Because there were more poor people than there were well-off people. They very soon realized that if you could read the contract you could bargain.

'Now, I understand that down the street there,' they would argue, 'the Janowscy, they are getting two *zloty* for a bundle of leather. And you're only offering me one.' Or something like that they would say.

Later the young shoemaker workers asked my mom to make a banner for the first of May. They wanted to march in the May Day Parade. And she did. Well, you have to hear how this story ended.

My mother was working with these young men teaching them how to read. The first of May was coming up and since they could now read they wanted to march with their own banner. She helped them make the banner and stood on the sidelines watching them march with the banner that said: Equal Pay.

But mounted police on horseback came to break up the demonstration. They were knocking demonstrators over, grabbing them by their collars, and dragging them away. The banner fell to the ground. My mother saw it from the sideline, picked it up and started marching.

And with all the bad luck she got arrested too and was taken to Radom, which was the county seat. Many of these protesters got sentences of ten years!' Ruth cried.

'Therefore, Tzipora and Matel, my mother's older sisters, went to Radom. They decided that they were going to represent Pola in court. They would depict her as their slow, youngest sister who didn't quite know what she was doing. That she was attracted by the colors, and the excitement, and therefore mistakenly picked up the banner but was totally oblivious of what it all meant.

She got released and they brought her back home. Her parents were ready to sit *shiva*!

You know, what you do when you sit *shiva*?'

'Yes, Ruth.'

'My mother was told that her parents were ready to sit *shiva*. Her parents were in total mourning. Grandpa Leib was so worried that his youngest daughter Pola would end up in prison and worse.

'She is my curse!' he cried, pacing nervously back and forth.'

But Ruth and I, there in her kitchen in New Jersey, felt very proud of her courageous mother.

Tziporah on left with diploma and sister Matel in Kozienice ca. 1918

'Now listen to this part of the story,' Ruth said with continued pride. 'My mother was now thirteen and the first of May was coming around again. The family was very worried about what trouble she was getting into this time.

My Grandmother Miriam pretended that she was fainting, and my grandfather called: 'Quick Pola, run down to the basement and bring up the raspberry wine!'

As soon as she hit the bottom step she heard the basement door slam shut. And a big piece of furniture was moved!' Ruth was laughing. 'She couldn't possibly force it to open. Everybody upstairs was laughing.'

Ruth remembered how furious her mother must have been.

'My grandmother, my grandfather, they were laughing, and her two brothers Maier and Daniel were laughing too. They had fooled my mother. She stayed in that basement the whole day and saw the May Day Parade only through a tiny basement window. She was probably standing on piled up boxes to reach the window,' Ruth said gleefully.

'My grandfather said that Pola was the most difficult child to raise. My mom was surely not obedient. But she achieved things, and so they knew she was dependable.

My memories of my mother are much stronger than my memories of my father. I lost him so early. But the few memories I have of my father also include memories of one of his apprentices, Maciek, who was instrumental to my survival.

He was my father's youngest apprentice. He was fourteen. Maciek, or rather Maciej, is like Matthew in English. He had a lot of younger siblings. He was the oldest. They lived with their grandparents. His mother was poor and widowed. She had five children. She had come back to her parents after the death of her husband.

Maciek's grandparents were poor old farmers. He had started to work as a young apprentice for my father, so one day he would find work. And he could take on the responsibility for the farm.

What a fun-loving fellow Maciek was! When you take in a boy as an apprentice – you get to know him very well. Maciek always gave me a piggyback ride. He liked to fool around. He would get one bucket of water from the pump in the courtyard, come back from my father's shop with the empty one, give me a piggyback ride, and check in with grandma.

He always helped her with whatever she needed. Her herb and flower garden needed to be watered, which was right outside of grandma's kitchen door.

In a way, I think, Maciek was my first love – one who gave me piggyback rides,' Ruth said smiling. 'He was like the bigger brother I never had. He called me Ruteczka. It means little Ruth. It's like a sweet nickname.

Perhaps he liked me, because he had three little sisters at home and he didn't see them. He must have missed his family – and me being little like one of his sisters … I really liked him.

To tell you more about Maciek,' Ruth went on, 'I will have to jump ahead, to after the liquidation of the ghetto; how Maciek helped me hiding from the Germans; and how he helped me join my mother in the first forced labor camp.

Before the liquidation of the ghetto my dad must have given him some money. He must have felt that perhaps he would need him later. Soon after the Germans had marched into Poland in September 1939, the order was that Christians could no longer work for Jews. That order came fast and furious.

Apprentices didn't get paid. They got room and board. They slept on top of my father's shop, in a loft, at the end of the courtyard. And they came to eat in grandma's kitchen.

I know Maciek didn't get paid. But what I heard later – I heard this while in hiding on his grandparents' farm, after the liquidation of the ghetto – is that he still had some *zloty*, and that he could use them to bribe the guards. My father must have given him some money. He must have felt that maybe he would need him.

Again, this is what I heard Maciek say: 'I still have some *zloty* from *Pan* Motek,' *Pan* meaning Mister. When I was living with them on their farm, that's what I remember, because I was listening so hard. I knew that they had to get rid of me. They just didn't know how.'

'How did you know, Ruth?'

'Oh, I knew it. The Germans had killed a whole Polish family because they found a Jewish boy there. They had come to search because someone must have said something; that maybe Maciek's grandparents were hiding a Jewish kid too.

During those six weeks when I was hidden in Maciek's grandparents' farm – I will tell you later how I got there, after I had escaped from the ghetto just before its liquidation – I was never allowed to go further than the barn. I could collect eggs and feed the cow. All the other children could run everywhere.'

'It was before the liquidation of the ghetto, I assume, that your mother had been taken away?'

'Yes. But you know, this deals with Maciek. I include him here, because he was like a family member to me.'

'And your father had been taken away by that time too?' I was still impatient to know.

'My father had been taken and all my uncles and adult male cousins, all the able-bodied males in the ghetto. I was about four years old then when I saw my father last.

But I have to get to Maciek!' Ruth exclaimed. 'It's his story. I knew Maciek. I was close to him. As I told you, he was like a brother to me. He was a country boy. He lived above my father's shop.

An apprenticeship is something like three or four years. I just don't remember his not being there. Let's put it that way. I don't know when he became an apprentice for my father. But I remember when he left. That was when we were forced into the ghetto.'

3

Kozienice Ghetto

'Later in my adult life I read that the ghetto was set up in the fall of 1940. It became fenced in only in the spring of 1942. The only way I as a child was aware of time, was that I recognized the seasons by the leaves on the trees or the snow on the ground. I lived protected within my grandparents' courtyard, which had a gate with a latch on it.

During the first months of occupation we lost all our furniture, because the order was that you had to hand over anything of value: your jewelry and furs and radios. I don't remember any danger to us. But I remember what happened to a friend of mine. Her mother didn't hand over her Persian lamb coat.

That was my first hanging. We all had to come to the market square, because there was going to be a public execution of all the people who hadn't handed over their valuables.

There was that family who had two boys and a little girl of my age. Their mother was my mother's friend. I played with her daughter very frequently.'

'The children were hanged too?'

'Yes, that's what I'm saying, my first hanging! I remember we all had to be there.

My father was holding me. He kept pushing my head into the hollow of his chest. 'Papa, you're hurting me,' I kept crying, trying to get my head loose.

But he didn't want me to see. He held my head with his hands. So that I couldn't move it, but eventually when he let go everybody was hanging. Everybody.'

Ruth was shaken as if the event were taking place today. 'There were about twenty, thirty people. I couldn't count. But I surely recognized my friend. I recognized her brothers – and her parents. That's a terrible thing for a three-year-old!'

'It's horrible, Ruth.'

Ruth just nodded. After a while she went on.

'That same week, I don't remember whether it was a day or two before, or a day or two after, the Germans came to our apartment. They decided that all the furniture from our apartment was going to the commandant's office.

Our apartment had very beautiful and modern furniture. When people came and they didn't know what they wanted, my father would suggest: 'Do you want to come over and look at our apartment? That could give you some ideas.'

My grandmother had mahogany velvet upholstery. We had furniture in pale blues and pale greens. I remember our couch. You see them today in magazines, this modern furniture, like a settee.

We had all kinds of beautiful inlaid chess tables and small little armchairs, very small compared to the clumsy old mahogany furniture from grandma. I was only familiar with grandma's and ours. Ours was like a different world.

They took absolutely everything, except my crib. Everything. Every chair, every table, everything! And stupid me shouted: 'Mama, we're common dirty Jews, why does the commandant want to sleep in your bed?'

Because they took the mattress too,' Ruth almost whispered. 'My mom hushed me. She was afraid I would get hit or worse.'

'They probably didn't hear it, Ruth.'

'Yeah, or they weren't paying attention. But my mom kept holding her hand over my mouth, because she was afraid. After they had left she was crying.

'Don't cry. I have enough lumber,' my dad said to calm her. 'I'll make you some new furniture.' But it never happened because other things kept happening. All that I remember.'

And as Ruth stared across the kitchen table at nothing, she uttered: 'This totally, totally empty apartment. Even the kitchen table and the four chairs. Everything they took, everything!

But my father did build a few benches.'

'You had to eat from a table.'

'We did everything in grandma's place at that point. She had the connecting door. She had all the old furniture they weren't interested in. And we took some bedding from her.

Once the ghetto started – that was, as I already said, in the fall of 1940 – they also began to bring in Jews from the villages and neighboring towns. Some parts of the ghetto, I think, mainly the intersections, were blocked temporarily with coiled barbed wire, and there were guards.

I'm not quite sure about the years exactly. The chronology of this time for me was only around events. But as an adult I later found out, that by

August 1942, a few weeks before the liquidation of the ghetto, some 13,000 more Jews from surrounding towns and villages were forced into the Kozienice ghetto, causing immense overcrowding.

They were bringing more Jews in after the ghetto was established. Many of them were relatives of my family. A lot of the Jews lived in the country.

Already at the very beginning the Germans began cleansing the countryside of Jews. If they didn't have a place to stay they were shipped further. We now know that 'further' meant Treblinka. They didn't know then what 'further' meant.

But my grandmother kept saying to these relatives: 'Come in, there is plenty of room.' We had plenty of empty floors of what had been our apartment!' Ruth exclaimed. 'There were even people sleeping up in the attic where grandma used to hang her laundry in the wintertime.'

'These were all relatives she took in?'

'Yes, they were somewhat related,' Ruth explained. 'I told you of my Grandma Miriam's sisters who lived in the country, and of their children and grandchildren. They were country Jews.

My grandparents took them all in. They were family. All of the old people, who didn't have the energy to come to town, they were shipped away. My grandmother's sisters didn't come. But their children, and their grandchildren came, all the relatives.

It's silly to say, but I was really very happy.

I had been an only child, always with adults. But now there were all these children moving in. At one time there were sixteen children in the house. Some were very young. Some were teenagers.'

'And you could play to your heart's delight.'

'Yes, I could play. I had cousins giving me piggyback rides.'

Of course, Ruth didn't realize how hard it was for the adults, particularly later on – the overcrowding, no place to sleep, little or no food, and devastating sicknesses.

Leaving Ruth that day and going back to the station I was imagining her in the overcrowded ghetto. She was only four and a half years old. She just wanted to play with all the newly arrived cousins she had never met before.

At this time, she couldn't have known that these families had been driven out of their communities surrounding Kozienice; that they had left everything behind, carrying only a bundle on their backs and the clothes they were wearing.

✶✶✶✶

And what did I understand myself, when in the morning of July 27, 1943, my mother with my two older brothers and me fled the gigantic fires of the Allies that would afflict our city Hamburg around midnight?

We children each carried a little bag, and my mother perhaps a suitcase with clothes for a few weeks' stay in a hotel at the Baltic Sea, only an hour train ride away from Hamburg.

The next day we all ran down to the beach. The sea was black, covered with soot from the burning fires in Hamburg. I pointed at the sky above. '*Mutti*, look how beautiful,' I exclaimed. 'It's all red.'

'That's our city burning,' my mother said, trying to hide her terror. 'The fires are reflected in the sky.'

Even my clever older brothers didn't scold me for calling that blood red sky beautiful. They just stood there with their mouths wide open.

∗∗∗∗

The next time Ruth continued to talk about the newly arrived relatives in the ghetto.

'Now my grandparents had to figure out how to feed everybody,' she told me. 'We had root cellars. Grandfather Leib had good customers. There was a sign on his shop, 'Luksenburg Hardware,' and there was a bell.

'I'll let word out, that there is a way to come and get stuff,' my grandfather said to my father. 'We have enough junk in those two cellars.'

There was one cellar and a second deeper one. But the customers had to figure out how to get there. Uncle Maier, the electrician, altered the bell, so it wasn't so obvious. My father was an artist, making secret doors, secret drawers for documents. He also made a very interesting trap door.

A bell would ring somewhere. That meant there was someone on the Christian side who wanted something. Usually it was a blacksmith, who needed supplies for shoeing his horses. Then you knew how to open this construction that my father had designed.

My grandfather would tell the customers: 'No money. Only food. I don't want any *zloty*.'

If they came with a bag of barley they would get whatever they needed, or if they came with carrots or whatever. If it was edible, goat cheese, anything that was edible.

One time it was almost hysterical!' Ruth cried amused. 'A peasant came with a side of bacon, some sort of a side of pork. I don't know. It was very fatty.

And my religious grandfather screamed: 'No, no, no!' But my uncle and my dad said: 'Yes, yes, yes! We can't eat it,' they explained, 'but we'll cook it with ash in the backyard. We'll make soap. Soap!'

That was like diamonds! When you deny people of basics like soap, if you don't give them any soap so they can clean themselves, can clean their clothes, wash their hair, that's dehumanizing! It's living like animals.

They made soap!' Ruth was very excited.

'They were educated people, my family. It didn't matter what kind of grain the peasants brought, because that nephew of Grandmother Miriam who had been a miller could turn anything into flour. He set up a little mill in the subbasement. My Uncle Maier wired it and the Germans couldn't find it. Now my grandmother could make noodles, pancakes, or whatever.

That's why we could survive because of the tremendous ingenuity of my family. There was an awful lot of skill and intelligence. If you ask me today how to make soap, I can't answer you.'

'I wouldn't know either, Ruth.'

'You need potash and fat,' she thought. 'I don't really know what proportions were needed for soap from that pork. But then they had something to bargain with, with other people who had something else. People will give you anything for a bar of soap.

Maybe they had something you needed. Perhaps they had some oil. It was trading, right? It was that kind of trading. And being right on the boundary of the ghetto, close to the Christian side . . .

Sometime at the end of 1940 and the beginning of 1941, as I remember, they took away most of the able-bodied men. 'As I told you,' Ruth said, moved, 'that was the last time I saw my father.

I remember they did mention a place where they took them. I found it on the map. I don't remember now but I found it on the map. Whether it's true – that's where they took them. That was what people said where they took the men. Which meant, maybe, anyone younger than forty.

My father was thirty-five when they took him away. It was a forced labor camp but I don't know what kind. It wasn't Pionki.

My mother went about a year later than my father. Because once they didn't have any more men to take, they started taking women like age eighteen, twenty, or twenty-five.

My mother was twenty-nine when she went to the camp,' Ruth said in a low voice, staring out of the kitchen window. 'Maybe she was thirty.'

'You stayed with your grandma then?'

'Yeah, because nobody wanted children. Children and old people were considered totally useless. And then little by little everybody left.

In the spring of 1942 they fenced in the ghetto, I already told you. They started boarding up the houses, their windows and doors. Our apartment became very unpleasant because it was now dark. Our windows had been facing front and side because we were in the corner. It became very dark. We were spending most of the time with grandma and grandpa.' Ruth fell silent for a while.

'The ultimate deportation to Treblinka came from Kozienice, because it had a train station,' Ruth continued in a matter-of-fact tone of voice.

'It was after the Wannsee Conference in January 1942, that gradually the Jews from the smaller towns and villages nearby had been brought to Kozienice and were deported from there to the gas chambers.'

That day Ruth walked me back to the station. She took my arm and after some time she said: 'I really think there are parallels between us in some mysterious ways.'

And she told me again, that she saw her father last when she was four years old, and that the Germans had taken him to the camps. 'Of course, I didn't know then that I would never see him again.'

After we had continued walking in silence for a while, Ruth wanted to know when I saw my father last.

✳✳✳✳

I was five, I told her. And I remembered my father coming to visit us the last time in Hödingen, a village in the eastern part of Germany where we had been evacuated.

It was only a short visit, perhaps a few hours, but I was allowed to sit on my father's lap. I remember that my mother asked me whether I didn't want to sit on her lap. 'No,' I said, 'I want to sit on *Vati's* lap.'

Later I often stood at our kitchen window, looking out onto the village road, waiting to hear the clacking of my father's boots on the cobbled stone. I never heard that sound again.

✳✳✳✳

'Sometime, still before my father and mother were taken away,' Ruth began at our next meeting, 'after another mass hanging in the ghetto the young people couldn't take it anymore and started throwing stones at the German soldiers. One soldier got killed. And that's when the order came. They killed two hundred teenagers from our town! The payment for the life of one German!' Ruth almost screamed.

'My cousin Chayah was killed in that group.'

Ruth pointed at one of the pictures she had again gathered on her kitchen table.

'Here, that's Chayah with her friends. She is in this other picture too.' Ruth pointed at another one, at a girl in a dark dress, showing her with a group of youngsters.

'My cousin Chayah was an orphan. She was the only child of one of my mother's older brothers,' she explained.

'Chayah's mother died in childbirth. Her father was then in the military but later died in an epidemic after World War I. It was the swine flu, I think. Grandma Miriam raised her, my cousin Chayah.

Everybody died except the one in the white dress. I don't know how she escaped, but she did.'

'They were all from your town?'

'Yes, they were local teenagers, Jewish, of course. Except for the one girl they all were shot, all those in the picture. In the town square, and we all had to watch.

In the picture they were just sitting around in the backyard of the birthday girl. It was her eighteenth birthday. The mother of the birthday girl had nothing to offer, nothing to celebrate with, just those few apples on the table from their apple tree. She probably said: 'We'll get together. We'll sit around in the yard and sing some songs.'

That was her last birthday. That was a birthday already in the ghetto. Nothing, nothing, they had nothing. They just had each other. Cousin Chayah died.' Ruth paused. She looked very tired now. It came close to the end of our session.

'Let's just go on until the time when you go to the first camp. I don't want you to get too exhausted, Ruth.'

'Yeah, at this point it was very sad.' She paused again. 'Because mom and Sarah – Sarah lied about her age. Sarah was very tall and lanky. You had to be fifteen to be considered able-bodied. She went with my mother, when they took the rest of the women.

Arbeit macht frei. They all believed it. They were so stupid!' Ruth exclaimed. 'Go and work.'

'They really believed it?'

Birthday party in Kozienice Ghetto ca. 1940 - 1942

'Yes, everybody believed it. They believed it. Otherwise there would have been an uprising a lot earlier.

Arbeit macht frei. OK people were saying: 'Look, we survived oppression under some of the Persians, under some of the Romans. We survived. There'll be hard years. There'll be hard times.' That was it.

I remember my father saying to my mother: 'They're not killing the whole world. Of course, it's terrible. But they are not killing the whole world.'

'They would've,' I said.

'Yeah, if they had been allowed to.

I remember these conversations because it was pretty dense for a while in my grandparents' house. Even though it was an enormous house. The whole tension of this house! Yes, the tension of it. And all these people together. The people, yes, they were related, but we would see them once a year normally or maybe not even that. We were now all together in my grandparents' house.

At one point we were – Ruth paused and then continued in a low voice – just my grandmother, my grandfather, and me. Just the three of us. Everybody else from the family was gone.'

'Nobody else was living there anymore?' I asked her.

'Not in my grandparents' house.'

'How did you deal with all this, Ruth? How could you manage within this turmoil: always changing situations, people coming, unknown to you before?'

'As I told you the edict that Jews could no longer work for Christians came early. Suddenly none of the Christians who had worked for my father could work any longer for him: the journeymen, I am talking about, and apprentices, Maciek being one of them; or the nanny who came in for a few hours a day to take care of me while my mother was in her shop. Also, I no longer saw the customers from the countryside come to my grandfather's hardware store, including the blacksmiths, and farmers who came on market day.

That whole group of people suddenly disappeared from my life. It was like a total shift, like an earthquake. It was as if these changes happened almost simultaneously. Everything that I was familiar with, people I knew, suddenly had disappeared within weeks. Other people kept coming in whom I didn't know. I felt totally disoriented.'

All these distant relatives who lived in the country around Kozienice within weeks came into her grandparents' house. 'Every nook and cranny were filled with people,' Ruth had told me. She felt that an oppressiveness had entered her surroundings. 'A sadness was hanging in the air,' as she called it. But after all the relatives had been taken away, she felt empty and lonely.

Did her grandparents choose to believe, as Ruth thought, that in the end they would be just taken for slave labor?

'Next door from my grandparents there were still a couple of sisters left. I'm not sure whether their mother was still there or not. I'm very foggy. But there were two sisters. They were the daughters of the leather shop owner. He and the boys had been taken away already.

Those sisters started a conversation with a German soldier. He was on guard duty. The older sister Ewa spoke German. He said something to the effect – I think he started talking to them, because they wouldn't have had the courage.

He said that he hated being there. That he had been accepted in the seminary, but that he had been drafted anyway. He hated to be there. I don't know what else they talked about or for how many days they talked.

Now, hold this. I have to go back a little bit,' Ruth explained. 'This particular evening, it was before the German soldier had told them that they were going to empty the ghetto the next morning; in other words, to send everybody to Treblinka.

I don't know whether they asked him if he could help them or that he volunteered. But it was agreed that he would distract the other two guards if they were willing to try to get away.

I'm not sure, because I wasn't privy to any of this, because this was happening next door. The older sister was already a young woman and the younger one was in her teens. She occasionally would come to see me in the courtyard.'

'What happened, Ruth?'

'Hold it. I'll get to it. This was just before *Sukkot,* the harvest festival. It is the holiday that comes after *Yom Kippur.* I remember it was on September 27, 1942.

Now, again let's first go back a week further. My Grandfather Leib tried to get to the synagogue for *Yom Kippur.* It was hard to get from one part of the ghetto to the other. But he tried to get to the synagogue. Any time you got out you never knew whether you would get beaten up or not.

He didn't make it to the synagogue, and it came to be that he got beaten up. He got beaten up so badly. They tore out half of his beard! Tore out half of his beard!' Ruth cried.

'That was to humiliate him. And it also caused pain, with the roots. He was bleeding when he came home. Grandma Miriam had to talk to him, calm him down, wash him off and bandage him. And she put him to bed.

The next morning grandpa could not talk. He must have had a stroke because his mouth was all crooked. We couldn't understand him. All this was really too much for me, because also grandpa, he wasn't really there anymore. You know what I am saying?'

'Yes, Ruth.'

'He was totally out of it. Grandma was trying to feed him water with a spoon.

But let's get back on track to the day before *Sukkot,* the harvest festival. It was twilight. It was twilight before a holiday. My grandma sat down where she normally would: at the western window looking out because she had to see the sunset. Of course, the window was now all bordered up.

She started to pray. I'll say it in English:

'God of Abraham,' and she said it again.

She was summoning God. And then she started pouring out her soul. I must have heard her do this a hundred times.' And then in a low voice

Ruth added: 'I don't know what got into me. I suddenly screamed: God is deaf! Stop talking to him! He is deaf!'

'You mean dead?'

'No, deaf! God! He is deaf. I wouldn't have dared to say God is dead. That brave I wasn't yet.

Grandma was begging him to protect each member of her family, especially the ones she had no idea about their whereabouts. Pola and Sarah were in Pionki. She knew that.

I started screaming again: 'Stop it! God is deaf!' She got so upset, my very, very religious grandma. She was angry and she cried: 'I don't ever want to hear those words cross your lips, ever for as long as I live.'

She was so angry. 'If we had soap I'd wash your mouth out with it,' she whispered.

At that point there was a knock at the door. And I figured, uh, I am saved. I didn't know what the knock was. It was the two sisters from next door. They came in, and they said to my grandma: 'We are trying to escape tonight. We want to take Ruthy with us.'

But she replied: 'Nobody takes Ruthy. Ruthy is all I have left. Nobody takes Ruthy.' She wouldn't listen to them, but they kept saying: 'We'll take Ruthy.'

And my grandma was holding me like this.' Ruth showed me. 'I was standing there and the minute they said they wanted to take me, she held me tightly in her arms and I couldn't move.

The sisters said: 'It's gonna be better. It's gonna be better. Let us take Ruthy.'

They didn't have the heart to tell her that the ghetto was going to be liquidated the following morning. They didn't know what that meant, but they must have felt something ominously terrifying.

One sister gently stroked grandma's arm. 'It'll be better,' she assured her. 'We know it's hard.' And the other one stroked the other arm, at which point grandma let go of me. The younger sister grabbed my arm and ran out with me.'

Ruth fell silent. She seemed overwhelmed. After some time, she said in a tired voice:

'I swear, I will never forget grandma's scream: 'Give me back the baby! Give me back the baby!'

Outside the sisters were pulling me, and we were running. We came to the gate. It was where the soldiers were. I don't know the name of the very young German soldier who helped us. He was going to light cigarettes for the other soldiers. He could see us. He had the guards facing him. And he was telling jokes, they were laughing.

That's how we got out under the barbed wire. Because that's where the gate was, you see? We couldn't get out when it was all boarded up. On top there was barbed wire all around the ghetto. But where the gate was, there was a little space under the barbed wire. We got out.

It was nighttime and we headed for the woods. Ewa, the older sister, carried me when I got tired. By the early morning – Ruth paused again and then continued – Ewa pointed to a farm. 'See that house there? That's Maciek's grandpa's farm. You'll go there. We're sure they'll take you in.'

I listened and I went. I didn't know where they went.'

'My stay at the farm was not too long. I'm not sure whether it was four weeks, or six. First the grandfather didn't want to take me. He complained: 'I already have too many mouths to feed. We just have enough food for our own family.'

But Maciek was begging his grandmother. He got down on his knees and kissed her hand, begging her to take Ruteczka in.' Ruth was very moved.

'His grandma quickly made up the story that I was Weronika. She said that they had a daughter in Warsaw who had two girls. And cousin Weronika, because there wasn't enough food in Warsaw, that's why the girl was here.

I was told I was Weronika. I slept with the other children. I was given chores on the farm, but only near the house. The other kids could go out in the fields. I could only feed the cow and collect eggs because that was not far away from the house.

One morning the grandmother said to me: 'Ruthy,' she quietly said, 'please don't call out in Yiddish at night. The other children might hear.'

I was dreaming in Yiddish. After that I was afraid to sleep. I was really afraid. Whenever I felt I was going to dream I forced myself to wake up. I don't know whether I was calling my mother or my grandmother. I don't even know what I was dreaming. But obviously the grandmother didn't want the other kids to hear that.

Well, things went on. They were poor peasants, I told you. We ate a lot of noodles. We had milk because they had a cow. And we had eggs from the chicken. She made noodles sometimes three times a day. But we ate.

The Germans found a Jewish boy on another farm. And they started looking everywhere. One day, I was feeding the cow, when two of the kids came running up the hill and they were yelling: 'The Germans are coming!'

Grandmother came running up, just grabbed me by the arm and pulled me into the kitchen. She opened the latch of the big baking oven and pushed me inside.'

'Oh, no!' I whispered and grabbed Ruth's hand.

'Thank God they opened the flue,' she said.

'The Germans tore the house apart. They were there God knows how long. They ripped off boards from the floor because they thought someone might be hiding under the floor.'

'How is this possible?' I exclaimed.

'They tore all the mattresses open!' Ruth was screaming now. 'They let me out of the oven when it was night.' Ruth paused again.

'And the house was such, such a wreck: unbelievable, broken dishes, broken cupboards. They must have pulled the tablecloth off the table and everything went on the floor: the dishes, the food, anything. It was as if a hurricane had gone through the house,' Ruth exclaimed. 'Of course, they hadn't opened the oven latch.

Everyone was grim, and everybody was quiet. There was nothing for supper. I think we had some hot water or something. I don't remember eating but I do remember drinking. The kids were sent to sleep and the grown-ups were having a meeting, which meant, grandma, grandpa, Maciek, and his mother.

I was sent in with the kids. But I couldn't sleep. I knew they had to get rid of me, but how? The other kids were sleeping and I crawled over to the door with my ear there, and I was listening.

I heard them discuss how to get rid of me. 'Well, we could drown her in the well,' someone suggested. 'No, we can't!' Maciek cried. And somebody else, I'm not sure who this was, suggested:

'Well, we could make a basket and you take her into the woods.' 'Oh, no!' Maciek cried again. 'And you take her far enough away so she can't find her way back.'

Like *Hänsel and Gretel*, I thought.

'First in the oven and now this! That's when I heard Maciek say: 'I still have some *zloty* from *Pan* Motek.' You know, from my father,' Ruth explained.

'I know where the women from Kozienice are,' I heard Maciek say. 'I'm sure her mother is there. They have Polish guards. Polish guards can be bribed. I have the *zloty*. I will walk with her through the forest so we're not seen, and I'll try to get her in to her mother. This way we can have a clear conscience.'

'That's what he did?'

Kozienice ghetto school 1940-1942 (Ruth front row, third from left)

'Yes, that's what he did. I don't know how long we walked through the forest the next day. We walked, I got tired and we sat down, then he would carry me a little. I was only five years old! Finally, we got there.

'We can't go now because it's still too light,' he explained to me. We were at the edge of the forest, sitting there and waiting for it to get twilight.

Then Maciek went over and talked to the Polish guards, and they obviously agreed. They dug a hole under the barbed wire, like for a dog. Maciek gave me a kiss on the cheek.

'Look for your mom,' he said. 'She's there.'

I tried to crawl under the barbed wire. He helped me, pushed me a bit and gave me a slap on my tush. And that's the last time I saw him.'

4

Forced Labor Camp Pionki

That day I was waiting at the station for the train to bring me back to New York. It was very cold. I pulled my coat tighter around me. Opposite above the parking lot a full moon hung in the sky. I thought of Ruth. I could imagine her by the light of the moon, creeping away from the barbed wire fence that surrounded the forced labor camp of Pionki, stumbling her way towards the barracks to look for her mother. I could sense her fear, but also the trust only a child can have in finding her mother.

At our next meeting, Ruth told me, that she wandered across the campground after Maciek left.

'It was all dark, I remember, no electrical lights, and by the light of a full moon, I crawled up the two steps of the first barrack. I tried to open the door. But a woman from the inside opened it for me.

'Oh, my God, a child,' the woman whispered. Of course, they didn't allow any children in that camp. The woman closed the door quietly behind me.

'I think you are Pola's child,' she said. 'Do you know your numbers?' 'Of course, I do. I went to the ghetto school!' I said. 'Sh!' The woman was pointing at the first door. 'This is one. Your mother is in number three.'

After a period of silence, Ruth said: 'And that's how I got reunited with my mother. I knocked on the door, and they opened the door. Of course, there were sixty women there, sixty women to a barrack.

This is what I think, the thing we can learn from the Holocaust. Nobody ever talks about this. The Germans used communal guilt. These women, the minute they let me in, were all guilty. Nobody snitched. Nobody snitched. They were taking on the communal guilt, because if I were ever found, everyone would have been punished.

Now, I think that is a very strong moral compass, which comes from the Jewish religion. Well, that's what Jesus tried to teach too. The strong moral compass is that you cannot do a thing like that, that you cannot even consider telling on someone. But nobody – three camps, several train transports – if I was found in any of those cars . . .'

'They would have been punished.'

'Yes, for knowing and not reporting. To me that – that's what my mother taught me. My mother taught me to be strong and to be moral.'

The Kozienice ghetto had been liquidated, and Maciek had smuggled me into the first forced labor camp, called Pionki, to join my mother. You remember, she and Sarah had been taken to that camp at least a year before the ghetto's liquidation. In Pionki and later in the two other camps my mother hid me,' Ruth told me. 'I slept on a *Pritsche* in sort of a hollow in the straw between my mother and Sarah.'

Ruth insisted that I use the German word *Pritsche,* meaning bunk, throughout her story, because that's how the women prisoners learned this word from the German guards when they arrived at a camp.

'They were pointed at and told which barrack and bunk they had to go to: *Baracke* such and such and *Pritsche* such and such.

At night on the *Pritsche* Sarah would pull up her knees creating a little *benkele*; I would put my tush on that little bench, and she snuggled close. We cuddled to keep warm and could fall asleep. We all huddled together in the straw. And my mom would also put her arm around the two of us.

Sarah and my mother shared their meager rations of food with me. From each one I took a little bit. The rations were not big enough to feed one person. But they each shared with me, because I was not entitled to anything. I did not officially exist. In the camps I did not exist.

In the ghetto I existed. I am on an official list of the ghetto of Kozienice with my name, my age – I was then three and a half years old – and my address. That list, established by the Jewish Council for the Germans, was found long after the war when someone was renovating one of the few remaining, dismantled houses in the former ghetto. But after the ghetto I was not supposed to exist.

There were so many circumstances in the camp where young women got sick, and my mother tried to nurse them back to health. Like one night in the first camp, in Pionki. There were so many insects. One of the girls, she was quite young, and she was there with two cousins, was crying:

'There is something in my ear. There's something in my ear.' But everybody was saying: 'Keep quiet. The rest of us need to sleep.' She didn't stop. Her cousins didn't get up. I am sure they didn't know what to do.

But my mother climbed down from the *Pritsche* and went over and asked her: 'Honey, tell me what's the trouble?'

'Something is crawling in my ear,' the girl cried. 'It hurts.'

My mother told her to turn her head. She spit into her ear, and kept turning her head. Finally, the damn thing came out. It was a bug. But the thing is, that there were sixty women in there. My mother was the only one who helped her,' Ruth said.

'When the Jewish holiday came, whatever that holiday was, I don't even know, two of the Orthodox girls had traded something with one of the guards to bring them a candle. They brought a candle to the barrack and they asked her: 'Pola, will you light the candle?'

'You guys know that I'm not Orthodox,' my mother replied. 'There are a couple of Orthodox women here.'

But they insisted: 'Pola, you're our mother. You are the mother of the barrack.'

My mother was about thirty-one years old. 'You're the mother of the barrack. When anyone of us is in trouble you're the mother. You must light the candle for all of us.' She knew the right prayer, and since it meant so much to them, that they had traded some food for that, perhaps a piece of bread, she lit the candle.

I, partly because of my mother's character and reputation, I benefited from that greatly. I also benefited by having her moral compass for my whole life. Under the worst of circumstances my mother raised two very good young women. My cousin Sarah had a very promising career. But she died very young.

Now let's go back again in time for a bit,' Ruth suggested. 'This is now 1942, because *Sukkot* was in September 1942. I still had four weeks or about six with the Polish family on the farm, and then went into Pionki.'

Ruth spread out a map on the kitchen table. She always had this map at hand during our meetings so she could show me where things were happening.

'Now, here we have a thousand lakes. I don't really know how many lakes there were. But there were a lot of lakes. It was woods and lakes. The Vistula was close to town. You could take a ferry into Warsaw on the Vistula. I don't know whether it went twice a day or more than that.

But I know my mother in her earlier years, when she went to shop for supplies, she sometimes went by ferry. Or else she went by train, because about two or three kilometers out of town was our train station.'

Suddenly Ruth gave a big laugh. She remembered when her Grandfather Leib would tell his favorite story to his grandchildren.

'I was a young man then,' he would say, 'when, for the first time, a train on its way to Warsaw pulled into the Kozienice railway station. For sure, I was there at the station, and up on that first train leaving for Warsaw. Then came this locomotive!' he cried. 'How scary and noisy it was. And all that steam. People waiting on the platform, their faces were all covered with soot. Of course, it was a steam engine.'

The older cousins must have heard the story many times,' Ruth felt. 'But the youngest, like me, we still were impressed and adored our adventurous grandfather.'

'What actually happened to your grandparents?' I asked Ruth, only realizing later how painful that memory was for her.

'The night I left, the next morning, they were taken to Treblinka,' she said quietly. 'And whether they went into the gas chambers that day or a day later, I don't know.' Then Ruth started crying, sobbing: 'That's the camp!' she screamed, uttering some words in Polish I didn't understand.

'That's where all the Jews from my town who hadn't been taken to forced labor camps went.' Ruth fell silent. After some time, she added: 'Into the gas chamber.'

When Ruth drove me back to the station that evening we both didn't talk. She seemed so fragile and small. As if she had never grown up since those years. I felt great pity for her, wanted to take her in my arms. When I waved her good-bye from the train, Ruth was already walking away towards the parking lot. She didn't turn around.

'How were you hidden away in Pionki,' I asked Ruth the next time we met. 'I understand that children were not allowed in the camp. What did you, as a five-year-old girl experience? You still lived in a child's world. Did it protect you in some ways? Or did it make you more vulnerable to camp life?'

'I believe not knowing the facts helped me survive. And my mother hid me as she hid me in the two subsequent camps. In the morning she would hollow out a space in the straw, because we slept on straw, and I had to go into that little space.

My mother and cousin Sarah shared a *Pritsche*. I told you already. She made sure it was the upper one. The only change she made after I showed up, was to trade from a lower to an upper *Pritsche*, because the lower bunk was more visible.

There was inspection every morning. There was inspection of the workers who were going to work outside. They had to line up, and after whatever inspection they went through they were dismissed, and sent to work. The barracks got inspected after that.

My mother would make a hollow in the straw. I would go in. She would cover it with the blanket, always made sure that it was like nice hospital corners, pulled very tightly.'

'Oh good, you had your own blanket.'

'Yes, we had a blanket. Well, everybody had brought something along. You had what you had. We had a blanket.

She made the hospital corners very tight so it looked like a beautifully made bed. Since it was above the height of an average person, you looked up and said it looks OK. You couldn't somehow tell if there was someone hidden.

However, my mother made sure to tell me that when the door opened, and I heard the clicking of the boots – German soldiers had taps on their boots, little taps so you could hear them coming – I was supposed to hold my breath. I remember asking how long and she looked at me – none of us had watches or clocks – 'as long as necessary.'

Then she corrected herself: 'As long as you hear any movement in the barrack you hold your breath so the blanket won't be moving. When you hear them go out' – the door would slam very loudly – 'then you can start breathing,' she said. 'But you can't get up because, just in case, they would come back in order to re-inspect.' I was told to stay there, comfortably breathing, maybe sleeping, and not come down for a long while.

Eventually I would crawl down. I would sit on the floor, and if I heard anything I was supposed to crawl under the lowest *Pritsche* and try to lie still under it, hopefully not to be noticed. And I got away with that.'

'They didn't have dogs?'

'They had dogs. But they didn't do their daily routine with dogs.'

'Oh, good.'

'This was getting the people – it was efficiency – getting the people to work. They made sure there wasn't something illicit going on in the barracks. It was like this quick inspection, going up and down the rows and out.

I would sit on the floor, and if I heard anything like footsteps nearby I would crawl under the bed. The beds were tall. In some camps there were two stories or three. But if you ask me now in which camp was which, I don't remember. I think I blocked a lot of it out.'

'I can imagine that, Ruth.'

'Yeah. The slamming of the door was my signal. But I could breathe. Because holding your breath for a long time is very hard, and I am sure I didn't always hold it. Maybe I was breathing very faintly through my mouth. I don't know, to tell you the truth. I tried very hard to hold my breath.'

'You were only five years old.'

'Yes, and that routine went on for about two and a half years there and in the other camps.'

'What did you do during the day?'

'It was mostly boring and somewhat scary. I was alone.' Ruth took a deep breath. 'When you're five or even five and a half, being alone is not great. I had nothing to do, and my stomach was usually grumbling. I played imaginary games in my head, what grandma would be cooking, what my mother would tell me tonight about our family.

The planks on the floor were not close together, at least not in the first camp, as I remember. I could see that there were rats underneath; instead of being afraid of them I almost considered them like pets. I would try to name them, like the one that had a white spot on its head or the one that had a very long tail.

I kind of recognized them. Maybe the way the shepherd recognizes his sheep I recognized the rats under the *Pritsche*.' Ruth laughed but then fell into a plaintive tone. 'They were the only companions I had most of the time. They were running in and out. The Pionki camp actually had no foundation. Under the floor there were posts of either stone or maybe brick at certain distances. There was space underneath.

Sometimes shacks are built that way. This was a quickly thrown together thing, because it was meant to be very temporary. It was not like the Czestochowa camp, which came later. That one had massive buildings like a prison.

These were built more like shacks. The wind actually came in through between the boards. No insulation on the floor, no insulation on the walls. It was scary. But there was no alternative. You just stayed there, and you obeyed. I got away with it.'

'What if you needed to go to the . . .'

'If I needed to go to the bathroom, so to speak? That was really a major undertaking. Because the latrines were right in the center of the camp,' Ruth explained. 'Which meant I would have to get out and I would have to be exposed.'

'Were all camps built like this?'

'The camps, I think, were more or less rectangular with a number of barracks, and with a number on the door of each barrack. Wooden buildings, in Pionki they were wooden buildings.'

'In the middle there were the latrines?'

'Yes, for all the barracks. Not much privacy. Sometimes I would just go out of the barrack and crawl under the barrack. Sometimes I would do that because I would wait and wait to see when I could find a time when it was clear, so to speak.

Most of these camps were supposedly empty. I am saying supposedly, because I wasn't supposed to be there.

All the inhabitants, all the legal inhabitants of that camp, were out working in the ammunition factory. The camp was empty, which meant two soldiers guarded an empty camp. They would meet each other on their way around, salute each other, and walk off in the opposite direction.'

'They would walk within that rectangle?'

'Yes, that's right. There were times I needed to do number two – urgently! I would just look and see. If I ran really fast and really low, they wouldn't see me. Because one soldier was walking this way, and one the other way, and when they got to a certain point they would meet and salute each other. That was the time I could make it.

But if I just needed to take a pee, as I told you, it was too risky to take such a big chance. And it was just simpler to quietly get out the door, do it quickly, and get back in quickly.'

'Ruth, it's just amazing. You were only a five-year-old child!'

'You had to. Or I had to. I don't know what other children did, who were hidden in that camp. I had to carefully calculate everything, because I had seen so many children killed in the ghetto. The will to live is very strong. I knew that if I were spotted I would be killed.

The only thing I worried about was not to be seen. It took sometimes an awful lot of plotting to go to the actual latrine. Sometimes I would decide it wasn't worth the trouble, and I was going to wait until it got really dark at night,' Ruth told me.

'Maybe I could hold it, because in the dark of the night, something that moves very low to the ground, it could be a cat, it could be a rat. You really had to move very quickly.'

'Weren't there also towers, and the guards in those towers would watch?'

'Towers were only in the more major camps. In Pionki, there were just these two guards. Even in the camps where there were guards on towers, what they were concentrating on was where the people were working, like in Skarzysko-Kamienna. That was my second camp.

The guards from the towers were watching the workers. Of course, they worked outside of the camp, inside of the factory. But someone might try to escape, for example. There were also prisoners moving things from one building to another, mostly ammunition.'

'The camp was usually assumed to be empty, right?'

'Right.' Ruth gave a deep sigh.

'You saw all this from a child's point of view.'

'Well, being a child, I didn't think of the bigger world. It's amazing how unaware I was of the outer world. I just knew it was dangerous, because if I got caught I'd be killed. I had seen people being killed for the slightest whim in the ghetto.

And certainly, being in a place you were not allowed to be in, was reason enough to be killed. Not to mention the fact that this was a place for able-bodied workers. No children allowed. I just was breaking the law by existing.

I tried to make an as small an impression of my existence as possible. Lie low. Play low. Your playmates are the rats. No toys. You can imagine them to be anything. And my imagination was good. I could imagine anything from any story I had ever heard, from all the stories my mother told me in the camps. But just don't be seen.'

✱✱✱✱

On the morning after I had been with Ruth, my husband and I were having breakfast in our apartment in Brooklyn. While sipping my tea I spotted two little girls sitting on the windowsill in the apartment building across the street, both with their backs to the windowpanes. They were talking to each other.

It seemed to me as if they were speaking in sign language, because I saw their hands move in front of their faces. Once in a while the one girl would lean her head against the other girl's shoulder. They were happy being together in their child's world.

As I looked up from our breakfast table again I saw the two little girls slip down from the windowsill, still gesticulating with their hands, and moving back into the apartment. Soon I could not see them anymore. And as I was thinking about Ruth my husband switched on the radio to listen to the news.

✱✱✱✱

I asked Ruth about the rats, the next time we met. 'They wouldn't attack you, would they?'

'No, they were just going for food. In the barracks there were wooden floors. The floor was held up by wooden posts, you know.

The rats probably could have easily gotten through the cracks between the planks of the floor. Or they could have even gotten up the three steps to the barrack and pushed their bodies underneath the door. There was an open space underneath the floor. That's where the rats lived.

I was never attacked by any of them. They were only going for food.'

'They would only attack people who are dying, who couldn't defend themselves, right? Rats are very intelligent.'

'I found that they were very intelligent,' Ruth said. 'They could get food where I couldn't. In the second camp, which was Skarzysko-Kamienna, I actually studied them carefully. I followed their example and managed to get food twice, but got caught the third time.'

'You did? What happened?'

'I . . .'

'No, Ruth, I think we'll go too far off track if we pursue this now.'

Ruth agreed. 'Let's just continue with Pionki then,' she suggested.

'How long were you in Pionki?'

'I was only in Pionki a very short time.'

'When did you go there exactly?'

'On the 27th of September I was with Maciek's family already. That was in 1942. The two sisters and I escaped from the ghetto the night before. On the 27th they liquidated the ghetto.'

'So only your grandmother and your grandfather were left.'

'That's right, from our family. But there were lots of other people. According to an article I read and talked to you about on the phone, they found about seventy to a hundred people who were able-bodied.

They didn't send this group to the Treblinka death camp, but they did send about 8,000 Jews from Kozienice and a nearby town. They sent the able-bodied to Pionki the next day. I was not aware of that, because I was still with Maciek.

I was not aware of a lot of things. I was aware of my mother, and Sarah, and all the women in our barrack. In retrospect I admire all of them. I am grateful to all of them. I don't know who survived, and who didn't. If they had said anything, I would have been taken out and shot. But they kept quiet. They kept the secret. If I were found probably all would have been punished, because it was very common, as I told you, to make everybody responsible. It was communal guilt.

I am very grateful to them. I am also grateful to the people in the railroad car, in which I was transported with my mother from Pionki to Skarzysko-Kamienna.'

'Did your mom carry you in a bag?' I asked. 'Or how did she hide you while travelling? Tell me about it.'

'Let me try to remember what happened. As I already told you I spent about four to six weeks with Maciek's family. It was fall. They would still walk outside. They had decided to get rid of me – because it was really unsafe for them to have me there. It must have been either very late October or early November 1942.

When the order came that the prisoners were going to be transported, it probably came about twenty to forty hours before. This was the time to load the trains. The order was that we were going to be transported, not told where or what, and that you could take one knapsack or one duffle bag.

My mother decided, that I was going in her knapsack. I was very undernourished. I was very tiny. I was probably the size of a two-year-old. Sort of bony little arms and bony little legs, just the size of my tiny body.

I'm a tiny woman now. At my tallest I was five foot one. And I have shrunk since.' Ruth laughed.

'That was my mother's decision. I was going to be in her knapsack. Therefore, I was going to be close to her.'

'She would carry you on her back?'

'On her back, close to her body. Sarah either had a knapsack or a duffle bag. I am not sure. To Pionki they came with more than one item, because they came from home, from Kozienice. We had our own blanket, as you know. But later they had to leave behind whatever wouldn't fit in. My mother decided the most important thing for her to carry was me.

She put me in her knapsack, filled in with clothes enough so that there would be no outline of my body. I was being packed like a little suitcase, of course, with some opening to breathe. I don't remember ever sweating.

Probably the train trips occurred in cold weather. When my mother put me on her back she told Sarah to pack in her bag everything as tightly as she could, because she was the one who took most of our belongings. My mom took me.

We had to go through a line of guards, and she carried me on to the train. Sarah marched behind her with whatever we owned. We were on the train what seemed to be forever, because the train would move, and then it would stop.'

In retrospect, Ruth pointed out to me at our next interview, that she knew what happened on that long train ride from Pionki to Skaryzsko-Kamienna. 'If a train needed to pass, they put us on the siding. Poland was still a functioning country. If a commuter train or a military train needed to pass, we would be put on the siding.

Although by distance, if I look at the map, it wasn't a tremendous area that we crossed. We went a distance that would probably take a few hours, had they not put us on sidings all the time. It took a few days to get there.'

'Did you get any food?'

'Nothing! The cars were packed with people and there was only standing. They stood the whole time.'

'For several days?'

'Probably something like that. Most likely people were leaning on each other and supporting each other.'

'And with you in your mother's knapsack. What if you needed to pee?'

'Well, yes. The fact is whatever happens, happens. That was my mother's answer.'

'Not any food or anything to drink?'

'Nothing. Nothing.' Ruth exclaimed. But then she added in a low voice: 'I was really quite happy. You know why I was happy? I could hear my mother's heart. I could actually feel my mother's heartbeat, because I was so close to her. She never took her knapsack off. Other people took their knapsacks off. They got tired of carrying them.

My mother made sure not to put her knapsack down. There was no place to sit anyway. The whole trip and nothing to eat, nothing to drink, nowhere to sit. When they got off the train she dragged herself with me in the knapsack to whatever quarters were assigned to her.

I had absolutely no fear on that train, because I was so accustomed to being alone. But now I wasn't alone. For me this was an improvement. Although it was winter I don't remember being cold. But you see, so many people bundled together. I guess the body heat helped.'

****

That night, taking the train back to New York, I remembered the train trip of July 1943. I was then three years old. My mother, my two older brothers, and I fled Hamburg in the morning of July 27 before the huge firestorm, which that night, and in the following days would kill roughly 40,000 civilians.

We were able to get on a train leaving first for the Baltic Sea and then, after a few weeks, for eastern Germany. We each had a seat. Perhaps I was sitting on my mother's lap.

'Why are all the houses destroyed?' I asked her, looking out of the window as the train was rumbling along through the summery landscape.

'That's the war,' my mother said. My brothers laughed.

'Don't you know?'

In most of the villages the train stopped, and refugees had to get off. The village people looked at us with mistrust, at the unwanted refugees from the bombed-out cities. They would have to share the scarce food they had. They would have to take us into their houses.

****

5

Forced Labor Camp Skarzysko-Kamienna

'We arrived in the next camp, Skarzysko-Kamienna, and were assigned barracks there. Again, my mother wanted the upper most bunk, the *Pritsche*, in a barrack so that I could hide.'

'Were you with the same group of women?' I asked.

'More or less, because as they came from the same place they kept close together; basically, they were the women from our town.

This camp was much larger. There were women from many other towns. It was not a makeshift operation like Pionki was, where really shacks were thrown up. Here the prisoners were again working in an ammunition factory. These were buildings, actually proper buildings with foundations.'

'Did the Polish manage the factory?'

'No, the Germans wrenched it away from them.' Ruth gave a short disapproving laugh.

'Now, some Holocaust survivors almost blame the Poles as much as the Germans for actions against the Jews. I don't, because of my own experiences. The Poles were suffering too.

When the Germans didn't have enough Jews for forced labor they took Poles. After that came the Slavs. The plan was, I learned later, to get as many years of forced labor out of the large Slavic population. But they too were considered an inferior race, according to the Nazis. The Slavs didn't just include Poles. They included the Czechs, Slovaks . . .'

'And Russians also, right?'

'Yes, and then there was also the war with Russia. But in the original plan of the Nazi regime, to dominate the whole of Europe, the Slavs were included as the labor that took over. The Jews had to be worked long enough until they were no longer useful, and there was death. Therefore, old people and children were considered useless, immediately.

Arbeit macht frei, was the saying in every camp, I learned way back in the ghetto. People actually believed that if they were linked to work, they would survive. Because Jews had been enslaved many times in many generations. And some people always survived.

Anyway, I need to interject the fact that there were quite a few Poles, especially in the smaller towns, who tried to hide neighbors, and helped neighbors. They took enormous risks. Sometimes they succeeded, and sometimes they didn't. When they didn't they paid with their lives.

Only a small percentage of the Jewish population in Poland survived. More Jews from small towns than from big cities survived, because it was easier to get into the countryside. It was easier to find a peasant who could hide you in a barn or some kind of place like that.'

'Like Maciek's grandparents did.'

'That's right. City people did not have as much contact with other people as did country people. If you lived in a big city you didn't exactly have a handy farmer, whose cows you could be milking for the duration of the war.'

When I called Ruth a week later, it was on New Year's Eve, I could sense she wasn't feeling well. 'My left eye is bothering me,' she complained. 'It's tearing constantly. I'm not walking around outside in the cold. I'm sitting in my warm comfortable house. There's no reason for my eye to tear. I will have to see the doctors again,' she said, resigned. 'My whole left side is bothering me. I have lost two teeth on that side.

But enough of that! How are you doing?'

Ruth never had complained to me before. I had an unpleasant feeling in my stomach. I started to worry about her. I knew she had cancer.

'I will slowly crumble away, I told my children,' she said. 'That's what's happening.'

'No, you're not. You are going to live on for years and years to come,' I tried to assure her.

'I spent my whole life feeling guilty,' Ruth went on after a moment of reflection. 'When I look at that picture taken of my class in the ghetto of Kozienice, I was the only child who survived. Why? Why me and not the others?

All the survivors, I think, probably all of them, feel guilty that they survived.'

'It's not your fault you survived, Ruth.' Was it God, I thought, who singled her out?

'There will never be an answer to that. I never wanted to be noticed in my adult life. I wanted to stay behind the scene, didn't want my name to be mentioned when later, for example, I organized tours for my husband Oscar and the other musicians. I did things in my life I didn't want credit for. When I look back now, I always hid under the radar, if you know what I mean.'

'Because it was dangerous for you as a child to be noticed. It meant death. You didn't exist in those Polish camps, you told me. It's stuck with you, Ruth. The fear when you crawled to the latrine in Pionki to relieve yourself under the eyes of the guards. The fear of being caught! The fear of being killed!

All that must have come up in your dreams later. You must have had terrible nightmares.'

'Oh, God, did I have nightmares. But there was always Oscar who would calm me when I jumped up from my bed in the middle of the night. 'You are not running away from the Germans, honey,' he would say. 'You are in America. You are no longer in Poland. You are with me.'

But now, as we talk, as all those times rise up in front of me, these nightmares are coming back. Why was I proud of being a Jew?' Ruth exclaimed. 'I didn't grow up religious. There was no reason. It was because of my mother's teaching me. Reciting Jewish poetry helped us through the struggles of the camps.'

And all of a sudden Ruth began reciting the Yiddish Partisan Song. Ruth told me that a young Jewish inmate in the Vilna ghetto, Hirsh Glick, had been inspired to write this song when he found out about the Warsaw Ghetto uprising.

I was moved hearing Ruth, with an air of defiance, recite this song, reciting it proudly – she, one of the survivors, whose hymn it became: a symbol of resistance against Nazi Germany's persecution of the Jews.

Feeling her strength and pride, I admired her for that, but at the same time I felt a great sadness about what had happened to her and her people.

'Is it right that I, being a German, a descendant of the people who had killed off almost your entire family, almost your entire people,' I asked her, 'that I'm the one, who's writing your story?'

'You can't paint a whole people with the same paintbrush, can you? You remember that German soldier who told the sisters, my neighbors, that the ghetto was being liquidated the next morning, and he would try to help them flee if they wanted to? He was one of my helpers in that 'gruesome fairy tale,' as you called it once.

About the exact circumstances I only found out later in Pionki,' Ruth explained to me. 'I only saw the German soldier, and that he could see us. I was terrified. That he actually was helping us I didn't know. My mother told me later. She had heard it from the two sisters who also ended up in Pionki, who had told her, and that I was with Maciek.'

Then Ruth told me a Jewish saying that goes like this: When you are a child your sins are taken up by your parents. Once you have your bar mitzvah you become responsible for your own sins, a coming of age, so to speak.

'I think I took up responsibility for my sins much earlier than that. But what sins did I commit then? Being a Jew – was that a sin?'

'In Skarzysko-Kamienna the women worked in a former Polish ammunition factory,' Ruth told me when I saw her again.

'When the Germans marched in, whether it had been Jewish property or Polish property, they'd declare: 'We are the conquerors and if there is anything, it's ours!'

Either they took it over completely, which they did here, or they left the Polish owner as the manager. Most of the time they would bring in their own. But that varied whether they had able-bodied people in Germany for that purpose or not.

The reason I'm mentioning this today is because in this particular camp the German commandant was probably somebody who was not considered able-bodied for military purposes. But because he was of high military rank, he was put in charge of a camp. He was able-bodied enough for that.

I'm assuming that he was crippled from the previous war or an accident or something, because I can only describe him as a severe hunchback. He was all bent over, and crippled in some way. But in order to maintain discipline, which his crippled body did not evoke from people, he had this enormous dog that to me looked like the size of a horse.

The dog's name was *Mensch* and for him a Jew was a *Hund* [dog]. His name was Bartenschlager. It's the only commandant whose name I know. I remember it because it is the only commandant I ever came face to face with. All the others were distant figures. And he had this enormous dog that was trained to do his master's bidding.

Every morning at inspection he would march up and down the line of people, I had heard from the women in the barrack. If anybody wasn't standing properly at attention, or whatever he considered an infraction, the command would be: '*Fass!* Attack!' Then the dog would attack that person.'

'What would he do?'

'Usually he would just go for the jugular. I'm not sure whether there was an extra command to make him do that or not, because I was never on the line out there. I was always hidden.

My mother tried to keep everything away from me. But, of course, I was very curious. I must have pricked up my ears to hear news from the outside world – even if it were gruesome or gloomy, even if I had no sense of its meaning.

In this camp,' Ruth continued, but then took a deep breath. . . . 'It was winter. It was cold. And when it's cold you are more aware of hunger. There was no heat. There was no hot tea, like we're drinking now. I was very much aware of the rats getting food and bringing it back.

And I made a study of the rats. I watched them carefully. I realized, that what they saw, I could not see from the distance, that the soldiers, who were guarding this purportedly empty camp, were eating something.

They were eating apples. If they didn't like an apple that was perhaps picked too early and was still green, they threw part of it uneaten away. Or they would drop an apple core, or dried up rinds of a sandwich.

The rats were bringing all this food back to right underneath the floor. I could see it through the cracks. And it looked good. I mean, once I saw part of an apple, and the rat had it.

Oh, you know!' Ruth cried excitedly. 'And I decided if the rats can do it, I should be able to do it.'

'That's what your mom would have told you.'

'Yes, my mom always said, I can learn how to do anything anyone else has learned how to do. Learn. Now, I wasn't a rat,' Ruth said laughing.

'But you learned it from the rats.'

'I learned from the rats. I mimicked them. I watched until the two soldiers saluted each other, and then passed each other.

There would be a period, where, if I ran fast, I would be coming in between where one guard was facing this way, and the other one was facing that way. I got there and hopefully there would be something edible. Because that's where the soldiers started out from, that's where they usually ended.

Well, I made it and brought back some dried-up rinds of a sandwich. They tasted great. A few days later I got brave enough and did it again.'

'What about the rats?'

'I don't know about them. I didn't have a discussion with them. I had the rinds. I had them. I don't know what they thought. There were a lot of them. And there was only one of me.

I did it again a couple of days later. I got a piece of an apple, a partially eaten apple. The third time I got caught.'

'What happened?'

'My timing had not been perfect. Maybe I ran too slowly on the way back. And, of course, I had heard about the hunchback and knew that the order *Fass!* meant an infraction. I feared the worst as the guards took me to Bartenschlager.'[1]

'That must have been terrible. What happened?'

'The guards were laughing because they had caught me. They got me because I was so little. How could they not have seen me all this time? They hadn't.'

Ruth took a break, then went on:

'They took me to him. He thought this was the funniest thing he could ever think of. He found it amusing that this little girl could outsmart everybody else. He thought it was funny. He couldn't stop laughing. But I was terrified, because I figured the dog would go for my jugular.

Instead, the orders were that the guards were to make sure that every time he had dinner that I was to be brought in to his quarters.

He didn't ask what my name was. He wanted *die Kleine mit den Locken* at his dinner table. The little girl with the curly hair. To him I was like – I don't know.'

'Like a mascot,' I suggested.

'Yes, a mascot, like the amusements that kings in olden days would have. Some dwarf or somebody like that.

He would sit down to dinner, and I would show up. I was told to sit on the floor on the left, and the dog was on the floor on the right. He would be eating whatever he had for dinner. He would take turns throwing bits of food to the dog and to me.

I ate every day. My mother and Sarah didn't have to share their ration with me.'

'Did he force you to catch it?'

'Well, he thought it was fun when I caught it – with my mouth. I tried. But when it dropped I picked it up so fast and pushed it in between my teeth. He thought it was funny. I was an amusement for him.'

'What about the dog?'

'He was a very obedient dog. I was terrified of him. But when he wasn't given orders to do something, he didn't do anything. He was just sitting there and I was sitting here. When I was told: 'Dismissed,' I left. And that was it.

He never asked anything. He never asked me anything. He never said anything that had anything to do with me as a person. I was just something that broke his monotony. It's the only thing I could think of.

My mother made sure that my *Locken* were like Shirley Temple's curls. She would comb my hair very carefully before I left. She was probably praying that I would return, because none of us knew what would happen. That's what was going on in this camp.'

'Ruth, when was it they caught you? Was it at the beginning of your time in Skarzysko-Kamienna?'

'Well, it may have been. I think it was wintertime. Maybe we had been there for two or three months or so. It took me some time to figure out the rats' route. So, I ate. That's all I can tell you.'

'I can imagine how worried your mother must have been.'

'My mother was very worried, I'm sure. On the other hand, when there was an order from the commandant, and they came to the barrack with the order to get me, every night. . . . Well, my mother said: 'You've got to go.'

Ruth laughed. 'Yes, that was the way it was.

Perhaps it went on for two or two and a half months. He never asked who my mother was. He never asked what barrack she was in. He didn't want to know anything.'

'Do you think that after a while you got used to being with that dog?'

Ruth pushed out a long sigh. 'It was routine,' she said. 'It was the routine of my miserable existence. But we still made sure that I was hidden for inspection.'

'Did the others know?'

'I don't know. I wasn't going to take a chance and neither was my mother. Maybe this was just a private thing between him and these two guards? We certainly weren't going to flaunt it. No.'

'It's incredible.'

'Yeah, we certainly weren't going to flaunt it.'

I could empathize with Ruth's terror, with her fear. Was it because I also experienced terror and fear as a child during the war in Hödingen?

✴✴✴✴

I remembered the day when I was locked in a stable together with a forced laborer. I was about five years old.

'He had a slimy face. I didn't trust him,' my mother said later when I had grown up and told her about him.

My mother insisted that they had been chicks. But I knew they were rabbits, just born, as the farmer's wife had told me. She called Pierre, or whatever his name was, to show me the newly born rabbits. He was a forced laborer from France who worked on this farm later in the war.

The farmer's wife and my mother went over to the farmhouse. 'They shot someone again, who tried to escape from the camp,' I heard my mother say.

Then Pierre took my hand. He walked with me to the stable across the courtyard. Inside he locked the big wooden gate behind us.

Much later I had a recurring dream: I open the gate of a stable and inside, deep down, as in a cave, I see rabbits, masses of newly born rabbits. The shock seeing them is so great that I scream *Mutti!* and wake up.

✳✳✳✳

'In the spring something was going on in the Skarzysko-Kamienna camp,' Ruth told me the next time we met.

'But of course, I didn't know then what was happening. In retrospect I realized that the Russians were moving up closer. But of course, I didn't know it at that time.'

'Your mother didn't know either?'

'Nobody knew. Nobody had radios. Nobody knew. But there was some kind of inspection from outside in this camp. Everybody was at work and they were searching the barracks. And I got trapped.'

'What happened, Ruth?'

'They found enough children to fill up a pickup truck. There we were all packed on a pickup truck.'

'And your mom was at work.'

'My mom was working in the ammunition factory. My mom didn't have the slightest idea what was going on,' Ruth exclaimed.

'They loaded us up. We were standing. We were packed on the pickup truck. I don't know whether it was the SS or what. They just came, and they inspected every barrack. They found a whole bunch of kids. They took us out of the camp and up on a hill. We were up on that hill, outside of the camp. And there were four, five Polish guys digging.'

'Oh, no!'

'There was only the driver, his assistant, and somebody with a gun, who was watching. There were just these three German soldiers. They were angry with the Polish guys. They probably called them lazy, it should have been finished, and all of that.

When they finished yelling they lit up cigarettes. They were sort of leaning on the cabin of the truck and smoking cigarettes.

I was in the back of the pickup truck. I was at the very end. I felt that I needed to try to get away,' Ruth said.

'Everybody on the truck – I don't think there was anybody older than eight. We were all very young children, small enough to be hidden.

Everyone was frozen with fear. And I somehow felt, I should try to get out of this.

I saw again one of them light cigarettes for the others, and they were watching, like hawks, where the Poles were digging. Nobody was looking at us.

I jumped. I don't know what propelled me. I just jumped. I ran. Stupid enough not to know where to run to, I ran back to the camp.'

'They didn't turn around and see you?'

'They were watching the Poles, and they were smoking! There were only three of them.

I just ran. Suddenly I noticed a woman in a blue cape. It was a nurse. She was walking on a path outside the camp's ground.

She saw me. Then she looked up, and saw the truck. At this point she opened her cape and looked directly at me. I ran towards her, and as I came close she said to me in Polish: 'Arms around my waist and legs up.'

A feeling of joy overwhelmed me when Ruth said these words, words that stuck in her mind and meant safety. I got up and hugged her. We both sobbed. Ruth was choking now, whispering something in Polish I couldn't understand.

After some time, Ruth was able to continue. 'The woman then closed her woolen cape. And she went back with me to the infirmary near the camp.

But why did she appear? There was that infirmary attached to the camp. Where was she going? Was she going home? Was she allowed to go home? I don't know.

For years I was thinking it was my grandma who sent an angel down. You know?' Ruth laughed.

'I'm not that religious. But then again – how else do you explain it? That she was just there, just at the right time?' Ruth got very emotional.

'I needed her! I needed her!' She screamed.

'So, I ran towards her.'

'Was the nurse the only person around, Ruth?'

'Yes, the only person around, and I had nowhere else to go. I mean, you don't run over to the gate of a camp with barbed wire around and say, let me in. And surely not when you are a little girl.

By this point I was probably six or six and a half. You just don't do that. There was a person opening her cape. That was a good sign. And the fact that she spoke to me in Polish which was my first language – that was it.

I believe that there is something good in everybody. The only thing we don't know is how to bring that good part out to nurture.'

'Perhaps in moments like this it comes out, Ruth.'

'Yes. The nurse saw the child alone. And she could make out what that meant.

When the women were let out from work, they were marched back to the camp. Once back in the camp every mother who had hidden a child, was crying, and wailing, and looking for her child. And so was my mother.'

Ruth was almost in tears. I grabbed her hands, tried to calm her.

'Of course, they couldn't find their children. Then Sarah said: 'We haven't looked in the infirmary.'

'Why would she be in the infirmary?' my mother asked.

'I don't know, but it's the only place we haven't looked,' Sarah suggested.

Finally, my mother went to the infirmary, and there I was.' Ruth was now sobbing._

'The Polish nurse actually was a Red Cross nurse with a blue cape and a red cross on the back of the cape. I later saw it,' Ruth told me as she tried to make it through this difficult memory.

'The woman didn't know what to do with me. She got me there. She had me there in the infirmary. There were a few people there. When my mother came in . . .' Ruth was crying now.

'Oh, God. And when my mother came in . . .' Ruth tried to control her emotions, sobbing. 'And then . . .'

'You were the only child left, Ruth.'

'Yes, that's it. I was the only child left. Now I am sure, I was the only child in this camp,' she said, still in tears. 'It was an outside group that was searching. It wasn't the person who was running the camp. It was probably the SS.

But this nurse kept looking at my mother, and all of a sudden, she said: 'I know you.'

My mother was not looking at her at first, because all she kept saying to me was, 'I love you. You know, I love you.' Ruth was still very moved as she continued: 'And then my mother kept saying: 'Thank you. Thank you so much. I can't thank you enough.'

But again, the nurse said: 'I know you.'

My mother looked at her and finally said: 'I don't know you.' 'Now I know from where I know you,' the nurse insisted. 'I bought a radio a long time ago. I bought a radio at your store in Kozienice. I only made two payments.'

Ruth was now laughing. She seemed relieved. 'Your radio is fully paid for!' my mother exclaimed.

Ruth continued to laugh. 'My mother couldn't think of what else to say, because she, of course, couldn't remember everyone who ever came into her store, and bought a radio.

You realize that the camp was still within, what in this country you would call, the same county. That's Radom. The Red Cross nurse was from that region.

She had obviously been from that general region. The only thing my mother could assure her of was: 'You don't owe me any money. You paid everything off.'

I had to hide again,' Ruth told me after some time.

'Did you continue to go to the commandant?'

'No. I was afraid to show up, and show that I was still there.'

'They didn't look for you?'

'No, they didn't, because they probably thought that all the children had been killed. Whether he had ever figured out who my mother was or not, I don't know. But when it was time to leave that camp, and go to the next one, he never stopped my mother. He didn't ask to look into her knapsack. She just marched on.'

'He was still there?'

'He was still there. Everybody passed inspection to get on the train.'

'Do you think he might have known?'

'Maybe he had selective amnesia,' Ruth suggested. 'Let's put it that way. That he just decided not to remember. Basically, I'm an optimist. I like to think there is something good in everybody. Perhaps the size of me had touched something in him. Perhaps he had a little girl. I don't know what to think of it.

He treated my mother like any other prisoner. He was not interested in what she had in her knapsack. They marched on to the next train for the next camp. That train ride was a much longer trip.'

Ruth pointed at the map spread out on the kitchen table.

'If you look at this map you can see that we went from Skarzysko-Kamienna to a completely different part of Poland, which was already near the German border. It had been Germany a long time ago and then it reverted to Poland.

When we came to the next camp we were still in Poland, but it was as near to the German border as could be. Here is Krakow, and here Katowice.'

Ruth located these cities on the map. 'If we are going in this direction – because Krakow was part of the Austro-Hungarian Empire, this whole lower part of Poland was part of the Austro-Hungarian Empire – then we come to another city.

That's where my father came from. Przemysl. Przemysl is now the last town in Poland before the Ukraine.'

'Well, Ruth, shall we stop for today? I think we both need a rest.'

'Yes, I think this is enough for today. It's enough.'

While Ruth was telling me her story, at times she got into quite an emotional state. There are a number of traumatic episodes that she retains – like her encounter with the dog *Mensch* and sharing dinner with the commandant, or when she jumped off the pickup truck outside the Skarzysko-Kamienna campground.

When Ruth told me these traumatic events she relived or re-enacted her memories of what had happened to her that day. The horror, the fear of near death clutched her and shook her in her kitchen, as it had in the camp.

I was a witness to these traumatic events myself. But I felt desperate because I was unable to help Ruth in her emotional state.

I also remembered that Ruth recently had an asthma attack, and her blood pressure went way up, so high she had to be taken to the hospital. Sometime later she threw up all her food before she went to bed, because, as she told me: 'Each time when I tell you my story, each time we meet, later in the night, I'm haunted by the ghosts of my past.

On the days when we talk,' Ruth said, 'I have a hard time going to sleep at night. There is a feeling I had long since put to rest. It's a certain kind of pounding in my heart, and a shortness of breath.'

'Ruth,' I suggested, 'perhaps we should stop it all.'

'No, no. We got to get it done. I actually talked to my physician, who recommended a lady who is a psychiatrist. I talked with her about it. When I started working with you. She agreed a hundred percent that yes, I must do this. She is willing to stand by me.'

****

That same night, as I was sleeping peacefully next to my husband, suddenly a fire engine with its wailing siren roared by our Brooklyn apartment and ripped me out of sleep. This wailing siren went right through me.

As so often when fire engines, ambulances, or police cars were plowing their way through the heavy traffic of New York, their wailing sirens would trigger a familiar feeling of dread deep down in me.

It's the fear of death from the war, when on any given night the sirens would alert us to the approaching Allied airplanes and rip us out of sleep. My mother would drag my two brothers and me out of bed, quickly dress us, and race with us, holding me in her arms, down into the basement.

There we sat cramped with other tenants of our apartment house – the children crying because they wanted to get back into their beds, and the women full of fears. They knew these explosive bombs could rip open the roof and would be followed by phosphorus bombs, setting the entire building on fire.

They knew that the basement was not a safe haven. It could, at any given moment, turn into a prison, where we would be trapped and burn alive, or suffocate from poisonous gas.

The fear of death my mother must have felt was shared by others: old people perhaps, neighbors, who were moaning or crying to themselves, and other mothers with their children; all listening out into the night, anticipating the approaching planes of the Allies.

All this I must have absorbed as an infant: my mother's fears and the fears and panic there in the basement. My mother could not protect us against such overwhelming feelings. She had to fight her own fears, her own panic to survive with her children.

And these fears, I realized, were ready to be let loose, when I heard the sirens wail through the night in Brooklyn.

****

I think I finally became aware that from diametrical positions Ruth and I shared the ghosts of our past: Ruth in her camps, I in my bombed-out city, and that these feelings are integral to our memory and our lives. They are indelible and continue to haunt us.

Even when not conscious, they are present – not simply images of the past, but real and tangible facts: whether it's Ruth remembering the panic on the day they had gathered all the hidden children in a pickup truck and driven them outside of the camp where Polish prisoners were already digging their collective grave . . . Or I remembering the panic we all felt in the basement of our apartment house in Hamburg when waiting for the approaching Allied airplanes . . .

I also have to agree with the novelist Rafik Schami, who claimed at a reading that 'children are the true losers of a war'.[2]

When on that day Ruth had told me about her escape from near death, I again suggested: 'Wouldn't it be better to leave these horrors where you experienced them?'

And while we were having tea, she reflected that she should really leave all that trash, yes, she called it 'trash'.

'For that's what it is,' she said. 'I should just leave it where it is. Back there in the camps in Poland.'

But then a smile came over her now flushed up face as she looked out of the window into her garden, and as if talking to someone out there, she said: 'I need to tell my story, before I die.'

One day I looked through different materials on the Holocaust I had gathered, among them books I had read a long time ago. But now, since I was working with Ruth, everything took on a different meaning.

I picked up a book of photographs depicting the persecution of the European Jews,[3] and while leafing through the book I was struck by one picture in particular: a picture showing a group of Jewish women.

They are stripped of their clothes before they are driven to their grave. It is winter. The women huddle together. The wind brushes through their thick black hair. Their white skin is glazed from the icy cold of the Polish winter. Naked, they stumble towards their execution.

I see the horror in their wide-open eyes. There are no words to describe that horror.

I remember Ruth telling me once on the phone, that she had sometimes witnessed a shooting in the camp – when she, lonely, and seemingly forgotten in the barrack during those long days, always scared but full of daring curiosity – peeked through a crack in the barrack door, although her mother strictly forbade this.

'I saw a prisoner, stripped naked, a mere walking corpse,' she said, 'who stood there trembling, and then I heard a shot, and saw the woman fall like a tree in front of the other lined-up prisoners.'

Terror-stricken she ran back to her bed, climbed up to the upper *Pritsche*, and rolled up in the straw. 'Why did they kill her?' she uttered. 'Had she stolen a piece of bread because she was hungry? Why do you have to die for being hungry?'

And she prayed for her mom to come back soon from work to the barrack that night. She had forgotten her hunger. Only the image of the naked, collapsing woman stayed with her.

When I went out to interview Ruth the next time – it was only a short meeting – she talked about why there were only certain incidents she could speak about, like jumping off the truck, because they stood out.

'It was different from the day-to-day routine of sheer boredom mixed with terror. On some days boredom just mixed with fear,' she explained.

'Boring gray days when all you felt was the cold and hunger. It doesn't make for a coherent story. It was just dull, and boring, and depressing. It even depresses me now, when I think of it.

The only things that I bring up as a highlight were sort of the highlights of my life in the barracks. That made something of a difference. Whether I lived or died, whether I got away from something, that was dangerous, or even when I got something edible to eat. That was a major highlight of my day.

My life was just grayness and boredom and fear, a lot of fear. Always fear. My mother, every time she left, she would say: '*Zey vorsechtig.*' She didn't say: I love you. She didn't give me any lectures. She didn't say, you must know the multiplication table when I come home – even though I knew it was the assignment she had given me the night before. But the one thing she said every day was:

'*Zey vorsechtig,*' which means: Be cautious. To be cautious meant different things on different days.

Sometimes I disobeyed because my hunger or my fear took over. That's when my incident with the commandant in Skarzysko-Kamienna happened, because of disobedience. I disobeyed. I left the safety or semi-safety of my barrack.

You see, my story was well hidden, because there were only a few things to suppress. The rest of it was so boring. It could be easily ignored.'

'To experience boredom as a child, twelve hours a day!' I said to Ruth.

'Every day, year after year,' she said in a sad voice.

At our following meeting in her house on Watchung Avenue I asked Ruth to talk about the trip from Skarzysko-Kamienna to Czestochowa.

'The routine was basically the same: Line up, either one knapsack or one duffle bag, and you march onto the train. My mother used the same system that she had used for the previous trip. I was in her knapsack. That was close to her body with some clothes on the outside so that there would not be the outlines of my body. Sarah packed whatever she could into her bag, and they marched single file onto the train.

I was on the train with my mother. Now, this was a somewhat longer trip. Whether we were on sidings more often for this one, or whether it was a longer route, I really can't tell you.

This train stopped many times, probably to let military trains or passenger trains pass. It felt as if we were being pulled over on sidings, and then being put back on the tracks.

We arrived in Czestochowa, disembarked, got assigned to a barrack, and the routine was the same. This was again a large ammunition factory. My mom actually for the first time mentioned the kind of work she was doing. 'So far this is the easiest job I've had since the war,' she explained. 'I can even sometimes sit down. I pack bullets in boxes. They come on a machine, and I am the one who packs.'

I don't remember whether she said ten or twelve bullets in a box. There was a little red felt thing that went into each box with the bullets. My mom didn't have the faintest idea why, but she was supposed to put this red felt thing in each box. And she had to do it fast.'

'Ruth, can I interrupt you? Could you first talk a bit more about how the trip to Czestochowa went? Do you remember?'

'What I remember is that I liked the trip, which sounds kind of stupid. I was so close to my mother, being right on her back, I felt her heart beat. It was so comforting. The train was cold.

It was either late fall or maybe early spring. I don't remember any snow when we got on the train.'

'Was that in 1944?'

'This was probably 44. In 1945 the war had already ended for us – on January 16, 1945 we were liberated by the Russians. I know that for sure. So, it had to be 44.'

'Did you get any food?'

'No food. No amenities of any kind, nothing. They just stood. It was cold. But it was always cold. It was long. I remember it being longer than the one before.

I remember the train getting put on sidings, as I told you, because you would feel the motion of the train going differently and standing for a while, hearing fast trains going by. That's why I'm assuming that they were either passenger trains or troop trains that were given priority.

Otherwise I got a certain amount of comfort out of being that close to my mother. I remember falling asleep, waking up. After all I wasn't standing. They were all standing. They must have been very tired. I was dozing off, and then suddenly waking, because I heard something.

Of course, I couldn't say anything, because I would have endangered the other women. If anyone knew that I was on the train, in that car, and the Germans found me, it would be communal guilt.

They knew, but they didn't report. I was always aware that I had to be very grateful to all the women who were in the same barrack with us. That they didn't snitch. I had to be especially good.'

'At that time, you were about eight years old already, right?'

'On that trip I was somewhere between seven and eight.

I turned eight in the spring of 1945, after we were liberated from Czestochowa.'

Notes

1. It was actually Paul Kühnemann and not Fritz Bartenschlager who was commandant of Camp A, Skarzsysko-Kamienna, where Ravina's mother and cousin were assigned. It seems likely that Ravina had often heard the name Bartenschlager in the barrack because of his notoriety as a rapist and murderer of Jewish girls as reported in Karay and other sources. He was 'the most dreaded of all' the officers who exploited their power, especially in sexual acts, Karay claims (p.80). According to Karay, Bartenschlager was second-in-command of the *Werkschutz*, the authority that controlled all three camps in Skarzysko (p.43). Kühnemann replaced Anton Ipfling in November 1943, Karay reports, and about his arrival in the camp she writes: 'As soon as the prisoners caught sight of their new commandant – short, chubby and hunchbacked – they immediately labeled him 'der *Hojker*' (the hunchback) and knew they were in for trouble' (p.122). Karay was an inmate of Skarzysko herself, ten years older than Ravina. She includes a song by a Jewish vendor that mentions Kühnemann's dog (pp.133-34). Abraham J. Peck provides another portrait of Kühnemann: 'There was Paul Kuhnemann, a lame, dwarflike man who, as commandant of Skarzysko-Kamienna Factory Camp A, would shoot Jewish prisoners for amusement, or allow his German shepherd dog to tear a prisoner to bits' (p.356).
2. 'Die Kinder sind die wahren Verlierer des Krieges.'
3. Schoenberner.

References

Karay, Felicja. *Death Comes in Yellow: Skarzysko-Kamienna Slave Labor Camp*. Translated by Sara Kitai. (London: Routledge, 2004).

Peck, Abraham J. 'Taking Leave of the Wrong Identities or An Inability to Mourn: Post-Holocaust Germans and Jews', in Alan L. Berger and Naomi Berger (eds), *Second Generation Voices: Reflections by Children of Holocaust Survivors and Perpetrators* (Syracuse, New York, Syracuse University Press, 2001).

Schami, Ravi. Reading. Literarisches Colloquium, Berlin, Germany. 5 November 2015.

Schoenberner, Gerhard. *Der Gelbe Stern: Die Judenverfolgung in Europa 1933-1945* (Frankfurt am Main: Fischer Taschenbuch Verlag, 1994).

6

Forced Labor Camp Czestochowa

'In Czestochowa the one thing I kept hearing, like the things you hear in the barrack – after all people were talking – was how much easier this commandant was than the previous one.

They were saying things like: 'He doesn't make us stand for an hour for nothing in the rain. He just marches up and down once, and he says, dismissed.'

That was like a gift from God almost, the fact that they didn't have to stand for long periods of time at attention in the cold before being marched off to hard labor.'

'For twelve hours probably?'

'Yes, for twelve hours, a twelve-hour shift.'

'Did they have a break?'

'In Czestochowa, I don't remember anyone ever mentioning a break. I don't know. I know that the meal you stood in line for was in the evening, at twilight. And, of course, I couldn't do that either. But I could peek through a crack in the door.

At this point, there was a lot of commotion; prisoners lining up, there were big containers of food, the prisoners were standing in line with their mess-tin in hand, waiting for the soup to be ladled out. I would peek to see where mom and Sarah or their friends would be on line; two women were friends of my mother.

There was a lot of hustle and bustle now; prisoners were pushing and shoving each other; everyone wanted to get in front of the line, where the soup would still be hot in the pot. It was about the only time that I more or less relaxed when they were on line for their food; getting off line, prisoners eating in different spots, standing, sitting.'

'But you were hungry too.'

'I was hungry, of course!' she exclaimed. 'I couldn't wait for my mom and Sarah to come back to the barrack to give me some food. I would gulp down some soup: two or three sips from my mother, and two or three from Sarah. Of course, I had to be aware not to eat too much, because they were hungry too. I also got a little piece of bread.

I specifically remember one time in that camp, when Sarah cried: 'Oh, my God, there's a worm in my soup!'

It must have been cabbage soup, and there was obviously a worm in it. My mother looked at it and said: 'Just eat it.'

I have never forgotten that. Whenever my kids said, yuk about any food, I would say: 'I have a story for you.'

They'd cry: 'We've heard it! We've heard it! All right, it's disgusting, mom, but we'll eat it.'

Sometimes I warmed up leftovers, and they didn't want it. But let's face it, my kids were not as spoiled as most American kids.

In Czestochowa, which wasn't as rigorously run as the previous camps, the commandant was a fairly elderly man,' Ruth went on.

'He was a high-ranking officer. He was probably retired and taken out of retirement, I understood from the women in the barrack, because it was getting towards the end of the war. They were short of able-bodied men, and they needed them. He was definitely beyond military service age.

Perhaps that's why he was more easygoing. Maybe he wasn't even a Nazi. He was just a military person,' Ruth felt. 'He seemed satisfied with the military routine of marching up inspections. He didn't have to level additional punishment on people. Maybe, I'm just conjecturing.

But the brutality of the camp continued in other ways. Once a week they would shoot the people who had collapsed, and were no longer able-bodied to work. Because they only kept Jews as long as they were able to work.

At one point, Sarah was getting very skinny and very frail,' Ruth said. 'And one day she collapsed in front of the machine. She was taken away.

Obviously, she was not considered able-bodied anymore. She probably collapsed from malnutrition. Sarah was taken to a barbed-wire enclosure with a roof, and it was open to the elements at least on two or perhaps three sides.

She didn't come home that night.

'What happened to Sarah?' I asked my mother.

'They took her away.' My mother was very sad. That evening she didn't tell me stories. She didn't sing to me, or anything. My mother was distraught.

But in the middle of the night she got up. 'I've got to do something,' she whispered. 'Just be quiet.' She left me.

Whether it was that same night or the next night that she left, or whether it took her longer to figure out what she was going to do, I don't know. But I think it was the next night. It wasn't that first night, because she was too discombobulated to even be thinking clearly.

My mother left quietly in the middle of the night. She took her ration of water, a little bit of water, a broken comb she still had, and two of these little red felt things, she had snitched from her packages.

While she was packing the bullets, it had occurred to her somehow at one point, that these felt things might come in handy. She stole one, and got away with it at inspection. And she stole some more. She took a big risk. She hid them in the straw.

That night, she took two of them. And she was gone. Outside she crawled on all fours, so she wouldn't be seen. She crawled to the barbed-wire enclosure where they kept all these people who would be executed, as rumors had it.

'Sarah,' she told me, 'looked awful.' My mom gave her a sip of water and said to her: 'We need the rest to wash you up and make you look good.'

Then she washed her face. She washed her hands with this little bit of water. 'Stop crying right now,' my mother told her. 'You are going to pay attention to everything I say. If you do everything I say, you'll live.'

But Sarah continued to cry: 'They are going to shoot me. I know they are going to shoot me.'

My mother reassured her: 'Sarah, you are going to listen, obey, and live. Stop crying now and listen.'

Then she combed her hair, and washed her face again. She spit on this red felt thing to put rouge on her cheeks. She rouged her cheeks with this felt thing, and she reddened her lips.

Later she told me, that while she was doing this, she wasn't even sure whether the color of the felt thing was toxic or not. But she wanted her to have pink lips, rosy cheeks, and hair combed.

My mother gave her orders: 'In the morning they are going to march you out. When they march you out, you know that you are going to live. You're going to walk out, no tears, head held very high, and shoulders back.

Don't look at anybody. Look straight ahead with head held high.' And she kept saying this to her: 'Remember, and you will live.'

Sarah always obeyed my mother. She did this time too. She walked out. They were walking them out. Some looked like walking dead. A guard came by Sarah and yelled: '*Raus!*' Out of the line!

Sarah looked healthy. Yes, she looked healthy. There was more work she could do.'

'And she found the barrack?'

'Of course, she was out, and so she was back at work, and back in the barrack that night.

My mother was right. 'Well, I stole once in my life, but it was worth it,' she said.' Ruth was laughing.

'Sarah was alive, but she was frail and weak. My mother insisted that now Sarah eat all her food. I shared with my mother. Sarah always had given me some of hers. But she was a growing girl.

I was hiding again. My life was as boring as could be. But Sarah was back. I remember it was very cold. It was wintertime.

One night my mom came home from work, carrying a package wrapped in brown wrapping paper with a string around it. She told me, that she didn't know, but at work her overseer, who was a *Volksdeutsche*, an ethnic German woman, just secretly put it down in her working place.

She was going up and down, and made sure that the women did all the work. Obviously, she thought mother was a good worker. I don't know what she thought. I don't know what she knew. But she knew something, because she gave her that thing wrapped in the brown paper – it was well-used brown paper wrapped with a string like a cross.

'My sister's children don't need this anymore,' the woman quickly said. My mother looked at her, but the guard turned away. She didn't want to meet my mother's eyes. My mother took it home.

A woolen sweater, boy's riding pants, and a hat.'

'Now you had some warm clothes.'

'In the nick of time. The prisoners, I might have told you, were forced to take off their clothes before their execution. The other prisoners had access to those clothes. Some rags from one of those clothes piles were wrapped around my feet, and the rags were stringed.'

'You had come from Kozienice ghetto in the fall. So of course, you didn't have any winter clothes, Ruth.'

'I didn't have any for years!

Years earlier than that, I had outgrown my shoes. First my mother cut out the toes. Then the bottom fell apart. For the last year or year and a half, there were just rags on my feet with strings around.

Suddenly I had something to cover my legs. I still needed the rags on my feet, because I had no shoes. But I had these boys' riding pants. They were big. And I had a sweater. It was brown. It was wool. It was warm,' Ruth remembered, pulling her woolen jacket tighter as she looked out the kitchen window.

I could sense what those warm clothes must have meant to Ruth in the camp. Particularly later, I thought – it happened before the day I was to come to see her in the morning – when her heart had temporarily stopped pumping blood in response to a surge of stress she had at night.

After a week her blood, even after much medication, still would not circulate down to her feet, making her toes turn blue and cold.

'They're icy-cold,' she told me on the phone, 'like during my childhood years in the camps. I felt the ice-cold, the frightening feeling of my toes being dead. I didn't think that this feeling would catch up with me again,' she said plaintively.

'I had long forgotten that feeling. It's awful.

As I'm talking to you,' Ruth said, 'I feel the cold in my bones. Right after we hang up, I will turn on the heat, although the thermostat is probably already on 69 Fahrenheit. The cold just grips me, and I have to turn the heat up even further. It would probably be too hot for you.'

Next time we met, Ruth described the last stages of her time in the Czestochowa camp: 'Time went on, and for me it was as boring as can be. I was hiding. I thought I was well hidden. But one morning this woman showed up in our barrack. She was obviously also a *Volksdeutsche*.

'Come with me,' she said to me. I didn't know what to do. I could tell she was a *Volksdeutsche*. Was that good or bad?' Ruth shrugged her shoulders. 'So, I went with her.

It turned out she was the housekeeper for the commandant. She took me out of the camp.'

'How did she know you were there?'

'I don't know. My mother even had a theory that maybe the few *Volksdeutsche*, working in the area, talked to each other. All I can tell you is, I don't know.

I do know, that she took me out of the camp, in the middle of the day, in broad daylight.'

'But someone could have seen you.'

'I guess she had permission to go in and out of the gate. I have never been smart enough to figure out this puzzle, because it seemed so out of the routine, and out of the ordinary.

She took me way out of the camp. We walked to the house of the commandant, and up to the attic, on a back staircase. In the dark I could see, that there was a very small round window on the top of the eave in the attic, and there was lots of straw on the floor. In the eaves there were three other children. I couldn't tell whether they were boys or girls.

'This is to all of you,' the woman explained to us. 'Once a day I'll bring in a basket of food. Here is a bucket. It's for your bodily functions. Nobody talks. Nobody moves. Nobody makes a sound.

The SS are coming. They are going to be here for a while. They are staying here in the house of the commandant. Nobody makes a sound.' She closed the door. And that was it.

Each one of us was in a separate corner. She kept her word. Once a day she took out the bucket, brought in a basket of food. We crawled over, took some of the food. We never said a word. There would be singing in the house, drunken laughter all night long. Day after day, I don't know how long it was.

Afterwards I was told, that the SS had been there for two weeks. You could have told me, it was two months. I didn't know.'

'And your mom, Ruth?'

'My mom didn't know what had happened.

It was a small round window at the top of the eave where hardly any light came in. We could only more or less tell that it was day or that it was night, because hardly any light came in.'

'You couldn't talk to each other at all?'

'We couldn't talk to each other. We didn't move.'

'Not even whisper?'

'Nothing. We were really scared. We were in different eaves, and in the center-part was where the bucket stood, and where she would bring in some food. She'd bring it in a basket, like a grocery shopping basket. That was it.

Word had gotten back to the German authorities that this commandant was running a very loose ship, in other words, the discipline was bad. That's what I had heard later.

They came to put the place in ship-shape. And they were partying in the evening. After that was over, after they had left, the woman took each of us back separately.

As she was walking me back to the barrack I looked up at her and asked: 'Why did he hide us?'

'He's a grandfather, he told me. That's why.'

'What did your mom say when you came home that night?'

'*Vu bist du geven?*' Where were you? my mom asked.

I told her. 'It never would have occurred to me!' she cried. It never would have occurred to her,' Ruth said with a broken, sad voice.

'How was it that you trusted the woman?'

'You became savvy, very fast. You could very quickly ascertain friend from foe. You knew, even the way she took me by the hand. She took me by the hand the way you take a child by the hand.

She didn't get at me, and grab me, like to pull out my arm, or by the elbow. But the way she took me by the hand. Come with me. '*Szybko! Szybko!*' which means quick.

Maybe she told the guard something, and there was one guard who – I don't know. Just so she could get in and out. But it was *Szybko!* I could barely move my legs fast enough to keep up with her. She was going!' Ruth laughed.

'So that was it.

And then I was back in the camp,' Ruth went on, 'barely got settled back in the ordinary routine, when a train arrived, and prisoners were ordered to line up to be shipped to Germany.' Ruth gave a big sigh.

'They loaded a train a day. It left and an empty one came back. That went on for about a week, or longer, maybe ten days. Make it ten days. The train got loaded every day, and then left.

I remember someone asking my mother, she was one of the women in our barrack: 'Why do you take the children and go to the back of the line every time?' My mother would let everybody go ahead. She kept Sarah and me back. '*Mir misen des oych iberkimmen*,' the woman said, which means, we have to survive this too.

But my mother answered: 'I don't know. Whatever they have prepared for me can wait. It can wait.' That was my mother's answer. '*Vos zey hobn forberayten, ken varten.*' Ruth had a good laugh.

'Now this was maybe on the following day. At twilight someone pointed out that there was some fire off in the distance. I don't know who said it, because everybody was outside. There was no train. And there was a fire off in the distance.

'Do you realize that there are no guards?' somebody else cried.

'They all had left?'

'Yeah, they had run away.

In retrospect I realize why they moved us from Skarzysko, which was a bigger camp, because the Russians were coming too close. They moved us to Czestochowa. They still wanted the labor.

Czestochowa was in the part of Poland that was near East Prussia. That area. That's where the *Volksdeutsche,* who gave my mom the warm children's clothes, must have come from. A lot of the population there was of German descent.

Now we knew, that there were no guards, that there was a fire off in the distance. Something was burning way in the distance. As we stood there, all stunned and in silence, we realized that there was noise with the fire.

The war was coming to us!' Ruth cried.

'That had to be the Russians then, because it was really quite off in the distance.

Then the communal thought was, my God, we are in an ammunition factory with electrified barbed wire. We don't need a full-fledged bomb. Anything incendiary that was here, would blow up.

The women now started running around in a panic, trying to see if there was a way to get out.

'Let's throw pebbles at the barbed wire!' someone cried. 'Let's see if there is any place where there are no sparks. That part is not electrified.' After doing that for a while, they found one small gate that was not electrified. The high elite used it going in and out of the camp.'

'The woman who took you to the commandant must have used it too.'

'You're right. Well, it just had a heavy bolt and a lock, and with pushing, with all the bodies pushing, it finally gave way. I think actually the hinges gave way, the bolt of the gate. But it came down, and we all ran out.

As we ran out we ran in the direction of the highway. When we got on the highway we realized that in the ditches, there were German soldiers in the snow, running away from the fires.

Now, we were running towards the fires. Our assumption was that running east was running towards liberation. The Russians were going to be our liberators, although they were coming very slowly.

My mother remembered passing German soldiers, and clearly hearing them say: 'They're running towards the Russians.' But they were in such a hurry. They didn't want to be seen. They didn't bother shooting us. They wanted to get away as fast as they could.

They were running west. We were running east. They were running in the ditches. We were running on the main highway. They didn't want to be seen. We wanted to be seen,' Ruth almost screamed, excited about their final freedom from their torturers.

7

On the Way Back to Kozienice

'I was with a large group of women running towards the east on the highway,' Ruth went on, 'and the first thing we saw was a train switching station down the hill.

It had lights on. We ran towards it. By this time, I think we were about forty. We ran down, and there stood a Polish man in front of the house. He was the switchman.

When he saw us, he screamed: '*Zydzi! Zydzi!*'

He started crossing himself, over and over again. *Zydzi* is the Polish word for Jews. We were so accustomed to Poles pronouncing the word *Zydzi* in an abusive way, as he did, that it didn't bother us.'

'He probably thought crossing himself would protect him, Ruth.'

'I don't know. But I believe he was praying for protection. He didn't know whether we intended to attack him. All we wanted was to get into the house. And there was that smell of food. He kept saying:

'You can't come in. The Germans were here. They just left. Their food is still cooking on the stove. They'll kill me if I let you in.'

It was like an invitation: 'Then we'll eat it!' Ruth almost shouted. 'If you're scared to stay with Jews, go and run away.'

'But the Germans will kill me!' he screamed.

'Run away. We're not going.' And he got pushed out, and we pushed in.

Now, I was not at the head. I don't know whether we forcefully pushed him out or whether he willingly left, because he felt the Germans might come back. He left. We stayed.

There were two black potbelly stoves, and each had a big pot on it, one with potatoes, and one with cabbage boiling. It was warm. There was electric light. We sat on the floor near the fire. We ate. We ate until there was no more food left.

It obviously had been a large contingent they were cooking for in these gigantic pots. At dawn he came back, and he told us, that the Russians were in town. The Germans had all retreated. At this point he was not crossing himself seeing us.

I don't know how many kilometers we were from town. The town wasn't visible. If the Russians were in town we were all ready to get on the road heading towards town, towards where there were people. We got on the road.

As we were walking, each time at a crossroad some people took off. Some ran off towards the north, because they knew where they had been in Czestochowa. Maybe they came from the north, like from Lodz or other cities. Some were going towards the south.

My mother, Sarah, Sabina, and I stayed together. We headed straight towards the east, toward Kozienice. The four of us suddenly found ourselves alone.

Sabina was my mother's childhood friend, and she had been with us in the camp the whole time,' Ruth explained.

'They were young married women then. There was a very close friendship. Sabina's husband was an attorney. She had a little boy of my age. She never saw her husband or her boy again.

After we had left the railroad station in the morning, at dawn, there was still very deep snow. It had been an unusually cold winter in Poland. There was a huge dark cloud in the distance hanging in the sky, which was the smoke from the fires we had seen. These fires were burning during the night when we had run out of the camp.

I also remember the gray slush in the camp in contrast to the white snow outside. We had to climb up the hill where the road was, trudging through deep snow to that major road which the German army had made.

Now, we were heading towards the town. There were ruins of houses on the side of the road – probably from previous attacks a year or two ago. There were also abandoned farm buildings: an eerie sight.

After a few hours of walking we met a man. He told us that there was still fighting going on in the city, but that the Germans had retreated. How could we translate this? Were the Russians now occupying the town, going from house to house, killing and looting?

Sarah and I just wanted to get home. We didn't want to go to the town. We were complaining about walking in the freezing cold, particularly me with only rags around my feet.

I remember well how my mom, every night, once we found some place to spend the night, would unwrap the rags around my feet and hang them up somewhere to dry. She would exhale the warm air from her mouth onto my foot while rubbing it. This way my feet wouldn't freeze.

My mom now insisted that we get home the shortest way, because anyone who survived, like my dad, aunts and uncles, and Sarah's parents might come home, and we would be reunited in Kozienice. Sarah and I surely needed some encouragement to keep going in the freezing cold.

It was getting twilight,' Ruth went on. 'We got to find a place to spend the night,' my mother said to Sabina. They started searching the horizon for any building that was standing. That was intact.

At one point we saw a farmhouse that had sort of half collapsed. We knocked at the door. A woman opened who I thought was an old woman. We found out that she had a sixteen-year-old daughter, and that there was just the two of them.

The woman couldn't have been very old. But she looked old to me. It was a peasant woman, with a scarf around her head. She looked very old and weary to me with hard, bony hands.

'It's cold. Come in. I don't have much of a house left,' she explained. 'Half of my house was hit by bombs. My husband and my sons were taken away a long time ago. There are just the two of us, me and my daughter. Come into the kitchen.'

It was a big country kitchen. She told us, that all she had were some potatoes. She obviously was a poor farm woman who was trying to keep her and her daughter alive. She was nice enough to let us in. My mother was very aware that this was a great kindness.

We probably were filthy. I am sure we were lice infected. I am sure we didn't smell very good. But she was kind enough to let us in.

We shared the potatoes, and we all lay down to sleep in the kitchen near the woodpile, near the fire, because that was the only room that was warm.

In the middle of the night there was banging on the door. A large contingent of Russian soldiers was crowding around the house, trying to get in. They wanted to be billeted. They were going to kill her only cow for food, her only cow that gave her milk.

It was rumored that the Russians did a lot of raping. They were much less disciplined. And – my mother had a brainstorm.

'*Bist meshugge?*' Sabina asked her. Are you crazy?

Guess what my mother was doing? She was reciting over and over: '*Amchu. Amchu.*'

Sabina knew what that word meant. And she kept asking: '*Bist meshugge?*' But my mother didn't stop.

The highest-ranking officer came over and whispered in Yiddish to my mother: 'They don't know I am a Jew. Don't let on, because I would lose all discipline if they knew.'

What my mother was saying in Hebrew was: Your people.[1] She said it over and over. It was customary when Jews were travelling, and they were strangers in the city, they would use that code word to find somebody.'

'So that's what your mom thought?'

'Yes, that was her instinct telling her. Then the officer shouted: 'The women go in the back room!'

The Polish peasant woman was shrewd. She knew my mother had pulled something off, and she came over to her, pleading: 'My daughter. Please, take my daughter.'

Polish and Russian have a lot of similarities, so the officer knew what she was saying. 'All the women!' he cried. 'You too, *Babushka!*' meaning grandmother.

The Russian soldiers ate. They made a lot of noise. The officer assigned a guard to the door. There were a couple of hundred soldiers. There was a guard at the back room. And some time in the late morning they were marched off.

That Polish woman was so grateful. She wanted to kiss my mother.' Ruth laughed. 'You know, she felt for doing a good deed, God had heard her. All she had left was her sixteen-year-old daughter.

The Russians had probably slaughtered her cow. They ate. They drank. We were locked in the back room. There was a guard at the door. We were all right.

It was January of 1945. My mom figured that if we get home, someone was going to be there. So anyway, we're marching home. And the frost!' Ruth exclaimed.

'Ah, Poland is very cold in the winter. At times there's a lot of snow. It can get down to 30, to 40 below zero Celsius. Yeah, Poland has very bitter winters.

We spent about two and a half weeks walking. We walked every day until twilight. At twilight we started knocking on doors. Sometimes they let us in. Sometimes they would tell us that we could sleep in the barn. Sometimes they would just look at us, and then close the door.

Actually, we were let in only twice. But the one thing I must say is, that we always had a roof over our head. We got some sort of shelter. Every night.

We walked for about two and a half weeks, not because we were that far away, but because it was hard to get anywhere. All the bridges had been bombed. When you came to those places you had to find out from local people where the ice was hard enough to cross the river.

'Is there some place along this river where people have put planks across?' We asked something like that. It always took time.

But the one thing I will always remember, as I already have said, we never spent a night in the freezing cold outside. We were freezing but every night someone gave us some form of shelter. Every night. Each time it was different.

I keep thinking: If some people knocked at my door, would I let them in? If those people were dirty and smelly, with their clothes ripped, and who hadn't had a bath in ages, would I let them in?'

'But Ruth, it was wartime!'

'Yes, it was war. Everyone reacted differently. Not everybody liked Jews that much. Not everybody let us into their house. You can sleep in the barn, they would say.'

'They could see you were Jews?'

'There was no question about that. We wore what we had in the camp. There was certainly no change of clothes. You had the clothes on from the camps.

We were not in camps where they had special uniforms. But you had to have a Jewish star on. We were imprisoned in camps where you had to wear your own clothes. And the only time you got some 'new' clothes was if they killed somebody.

This way, I already told you, people could get their clothes. You could get a worn sweater or something – from a dead person. Ah.' Ruth gave an angry sigh.

'Or a pair of shoes.'

I looked at her. I wanted to say something, how sorry I was, how dreadful all this was. Was it too overwhelming for me to respond? Did I feel ashamed for being German?

After some time, Ruth went on: 'At one point, people let us into their farmhouse. This was actually the second time someone let us into the house. 'It's warm in the kitchen,' they said.

They put some straw on the floor. And they let us sleep in the kitchen, which was very nice and warm.

Next morning, we woke up to the smell of some very good food. The peasant woman was cooking, and it just smelled so delicious,' Ruth exclaimed.

'We realized, of course, she wasn't cooking for us.

'I have guests, paying guests upstairs,' she explained to us. She was cooking breakfast for them.

They were four strong men, healthy looking – at least to me, because I was only used to seeing people in the camps that were skin and bones. These men came down, and they sat down at the kitchen table.

She was serving them eggs and bacon. She put a whole round Polish black bread on the table, and also homemade, freshly churned butter in the shape of an egg.

I had never seen things like this, never smelled anything like this: the smell of the baking of bread, the smell of frying bacon. Grandma Miriam would buy bread from the baker in town.

I went over to the table with my mouth wide open. I was so little. My chin didn't even reach the table. I stood there staring at the food.

And one of the men took a big chunk of bread, just cut it with his knife, and put a slab of butter on it. I must say a slab of butter, and he said to me: 'Eat. Maybe, some day you will be my daughter-in-law. When I left to join the underground, I left a boy your size.'

'How nice of him to say that, Ruth.'

'Yes. Well, this was the first time I remember eating butter,' Ruth almost whispered. 'Maybe when I was a child there was butter in the house and also bread; but of course, not in the ghetto.

Today I am addicted to butter. Butter is an obsession with me. I don't care. If I have nothing else in the house, if I have bread and butter, I'm fine.'

Ruth had a good laugh remembering that delicious, freshly baked bread in the peasant woman's house in Poland. She also remembered sitting on the floor by the wood fire, and she, her mother, Sarah, and Sabina holding a cup of warm tea in their hands.

'I am remembering these things. She didn't give us bread with butter. She probably gave us bread from the day before. And she gave us hot tea to warm up. We didn't get the butter.

But I got the butter,' Ruth insisted. 'And it has stuck with me.

This was January 1945. Today I cook with oil, but I eat butter. Bread and butter that is the staff of life for me.' Ruth laughed again.

'It made that kind of an imprint. And I'm telling you, this was not just a little piece of bread. She baked a large loaf, and it was on the table on a board with a knife.

He just cut a big chunk of bread and put a slab of butter on it. It was heaven. You may keep your caviar or whatever. For me bread and butter – that is my idea of the most heavenly food there is.'

****

When I took the train back to New York that evening I remembered that cold winter of 1944/45 in Hödingen toward the end of the war. There was no wood to heat the two rooms we were given in the farmhouse in that village.

My mother had been roaming through the fields and forests, looking for some wood, when one day she discovered a lookout tower on a forest clearing.

Together with another refugee woman from our town, her three girls and the three of us, the women set out to saw down the wooden lookout tower that promised heat.

The two mothers had started to saw, and we children were gathering twigs for heating. All around the snow glittered in the sun.

All of a sudden, a group of Russian soldiers appeared. We children saw them approaching, coming toward us, trudging through the snow-covered clearing.

They grabbed our mothers, ripped them away from their sawing work, and pushed them back to the edge of the forest. Our mothers didn't cry or utter a word. And we couldn't understand what was happening to them.

We stared at the traces of our mothers' dragging feet in the snow leading away from us. And suddenly, as if the icy spell that had fallen upon us was lifted, we started to scream.

We screamed for our mothers to come back. And, as if God had heard the children cry, there was suddenly a shrill whistle across the clearing. A Russian officer came running from the other edge of the forest toward the group of soldiers. And he sent back our mothers.

We saw them coming toward us; trudging through the deep snow. They were pale, and trembling, and with dread looks in their eyes.

✳✳✳✳

Note

1.   'As regards *'Amcha, El!,'* you may recall my acknowledgment in a previous email of being unfamiliar with this expression as a signal of one's identity between Jews, which is why I tend to agree with Barbara [Wind] that the 'code word' used for this purpose was different. But I have to wonder about *'Amchu.'* It might be helpful here to explain that a possessive pronoun in Hebrew usually takes the form of a suffix attached to a noun it applies to. Thus, *'am'* is the word for 'people,' *'ami'* is 'my people,' *'amcho'* (or *'amcha'*)

is 'your people.' It's possible that many survivors weren't all that familiar with Hebrew, so that *'amcho/a'* was slightly altered to *'amchu,'* and this became the prevailing form . . . .' (Mel Rosenthal, email to the author, 11 January 2015).

Reference

Rosenthal, Mel. Email to the author. 11 January 2015.

8

Back in Kozienice

'Finally, we came back to Kozienice. As I told you, it took us about two and a half weeks. We could only walk for about three or four hours, in the warmth of the day. Then we started knocking on doors, often of partly destroyed houses. Sometimes that process could take three hours until we would find a place to stay.

It shouldn't have taken that long to get back to Kozienice, but none of the bridges were standing. Every river and every brook you had to figure out how to cross. I also mentioned that before. You would ask some peasant:

'Is there a bridge upstream? Is there a bridge downstream?' We should go down another quarter of a kilometer where people have put planks over rocks, they'd answer.

We were really zigzagging,' Ruth added. 'But we were going in the right general direction.'

At our next meeting, on her return to Kozienice Ruth described the sad state of the town: 'Kozienice was partially bombed – of the ghetto there wasn't much left.'

'Was it also bombed?'

'The ghetto wasn't really bombed. It was dismantled, that's what I'd say. We were the first people to arrive. We were the first four Jews to arrive in Kozienice.

Then the next was a man. He came alone, and I thought he was ancient. He was fifty years old. And he made it home. Then there were five of us.

The ghetto had been dismantled right after it was liquidated, we found out later. That was a good chunk of the town.

By the summer of 1944, because of the advancing Russian army from the east side of the Vistula, the German army gave an order that all people from towns closer to the Vistula had to move out,' Ruth told me.

'This rather large area was cleared and turned into a no man's land. That's where the farm of Maciek's grandparents was. And that's why they were forced to leave their farm. My mother made a great effort to learn about Maciek and his family.

She found out from peasants, who had come back after the war to claim their vacant land, that he and his younger brother, had been taken away by the Germans for forced labor.

Later, during the clearing, his grandfather, while packing up the wagon to leave, suddenly collapsed and died. The Germans gave the family permission to bury him on his land.

After that his grandmother, his mother, and the three little sisters left with the wagon. None of the former neighbors could give my mother news about the whereabouts of Maciek and the rest of his family.

Some of the houses in town had suffered from bombing. But that was not the worst of it; also, vandalism, God knows what,' Ruth continued.

'I remember distinctly, that the convent was still standing, and two churches. The town hall complex was there and the hospital at the other end of town. One of the business streets looked as if hooligans had gone through it. It was one of the elegant streets.'

'That's where your mother had her store.'

'Yes, my mother had her store there. The pub was still open. The owner had been her landlord. The first thing he asked her after we had arrived: 'Pola, you are going to open business again?'

My mother thought that he was crazy.' Ruth was laughing.

'I doubt it,' my mother answered. 'Anything I can do for you?' he asked her. 'Some food would be nice.'

He gave us these big sandwiches, and my mother started talking to him about where one could go to sleep.

'Go a little beyond the main fountain,' the pub owner explained. 'There are still people living there. People you went to school with.'

Anyway, we ended up in the kitchen of a young woman who had gone to school with my mother. She let us stay in the kitchen. We were four with Sabina. She told us, she had no other room in the rest of the house, because she had taken in relatives who lost their homes.

We stayed in the kitchen there for a few days. It was not great.'

'But you got some food?'

'We got some food somehow or other. I really don't even know how. There was food, but it all was in bad shape, because the town had been vacated. The people were told to leave, or ordered to leave during the fighting.

The root vegetable had frozen. You had frozen potatoes, frozen carrots. They mostly tasted watery and tasteless. But it was food. We ate it. They shared with us what they had. Some people had some barley. It was a meager existence for everyone we came across.'

****

As Ruth was preparing some tea for us I thought of Hödingen, right after the war, how one of my brothers and I, because we were always hungry, went to the edge of the village. We dug out potatoes, washed them in the creek nearby, and ate them right there.

We believed it to be a most delicious meal, particularly eating them in secret, hidden from the farmer.

Another time – I was about six years old – I was even luckier to get some food. When the Russian occupying forces came to our village a contingent of soldiers had taken quarters in our farmhouse.

One day my mother said to me: 'I smell potato pancakes. The farmer's wife must have baked potato pancakes for the Russians. Run down and sing and dance for the soldiers. I'm sure they'll give you some pancakes.'

I was excited about getting some potato pancakes. So, I followed the good smells down to the farmer's sitting room. The door stood wide open. The soldiers were feasting on those pancakes and drinking potato *schnaps*.

'I'll sing and dance for you,' I said, standing at the doorstep, hoping that some potato pancakes would still be left.

The soldiers laughed. 'Come on in,' they shouted.

One soldier picked me up and put me on the farmer's dining table. Others shoved the empty plates and glasses to the side. They fell off the table and lay smashed in pieces on the floor.

'Dance little girl,' they cried, clapping with their hands, first slowly then faster and faster.

I began to dance, turning around and around in my little red skirt, dancing to the rhythm of their clapping hands.

'Sing, little girl,' they cried. And I started to sing the song about the ladybug and the father who was in the war: '*Maikäfer flieg, dein Vater ist im Krieg . . .*' Little ladybug go fly, your father is in the war . . .

One soldier sat me down on his soldier's legs. He fed me some delicious potato pancakes fried in *speck*. Greedily I wolfed them down. The soldiers thought that this was great fun. They were howling with joy and drunkenness.

Another soldier took me and pressed me to his sweaty, hairy chest. I felt his hot breath on my face and smelled the potato *schnaps*, which the farmer's wife had to serve them.

****

'My mother went to the town hall in Kozienice right away,' Ruth told me, when we met next time.

'She registered us in Kozienice. We were back. She tried to find out whether there were any Jewish properties still standing.

It seemed that there was only one. It wasn't very far from the convent. They were using it for homeless Polish families. It was rather a nice property of a wealthy Jewish family. She knew the name of that family.

My mother right away started negotiating: 'Every day another Jew is coming back – first we were five, then seven,' my mother explained. 'And we all are sleeping on floors in people's houses. Therefore, this house should be designated as our property.'

My mom was willing to run it in the name of the family. I don't remember the name, but she knew the family. She knew how many children they had.

But the town officials couldn't take any action.

'After all, the house is being utilized by the convent for these families,' they said. 'They are homeless.'

'The convent is very large,' my mother argued. 'I'm sure they can accommodate these few homeless families. But we Jews have no place to go, absolutely no place.

You know that the other small towns around Kozienice were liquidated during the war. They brought those Jews into our ghetto.

We can't go there,' she insisted. 'There are no houses left. This house is ours. We should have it.'

It wasn't easy negotiating. They were saying, well – this, that, and the other thing.

It all of a sudden occurred to my mother that the contingent of Russians that were billeted near the hospital had three Jewish soldiers. She knew it was three, because one of them was a local boy, who had run away to Russia when the Germans were approaching. He had come back. He brought these two friends, to meet the few Jews left in our town.

My mother knew he was there! Ruth exclaimed, half laughing.

'You don't want me to involve the Russians in this, do you?' she asked them.

'Oh, no!' the town officials cried. 'We had enough with the Germans. Let's not start with the Russians.

Well, look. We've got these barrels of mail,' they suggested to her. 'The letters are all to Jews.'

Of course, my mother knew where they were going.

'We don't know what to do with them. Will you be the Jewish postmistress?'

My mother was delighted. She promised that she was going to answer every letter. And she did. Every single one. Mostly they were from Jews in foreign countries, who had relatives in Kozienice. They were writing to their relatives to find out if they had survived.

My mother felt it to be a noble cause to let them know the yes or no. In some instances, she knew details, for example, what year they died, when they were taken away. If there was anything extra to say, she would say it. Some of them were even so grateful that my mother got mail back.

One day she got a letter back from a Jewish family in Brazil, whom she had reported to. There was a photograph of a husband and his wife and their three little boys. It was a very nice photograph of the family, but it annoyed my mother somehow.

She wasn't even sure why, because the husband didn't say anything in the letter to her. Did he want to impress her? All what the former shoemaker's son could say, was, thank you for your kindness.

But Sarah, being artistic, kept playing with it. She suggested that the family went through a lot of trouble. They went to a photographer and dressed up in costumes to show that they were wealthy. The wife was wearing three strands of pearls.

They were probably fake pearls,' Ruth thought. 'He was wearing something like a tuxedo, and the little boys also were all dressed up.

Sarah felt that there was something there. They started playing with it. And as they were playing with the photograph, it came apart. There was a fake other side where the dedication was, and in between lay a hundred dollars.

That's why the sender went through all this artifice, so we wouldn't just think this was only a photograph,' Ruth exclaimed. 'He was from Kozienice. He knew Pola. He knew the Luksenburgs. He thought they would figure it out. It was illegal to send money. Dollars, a hundred dollars!'

'That was a lot of money in those days, Ruth.'

'That was enough to keep the little Jewish community alive. At this point, there were maybe twenty-eight going on thirty. And it would pay for food for a long time.'

'Did Pola finally get the house?'

'She got the house. This is why she became postmistress in town. She was writing to everyone, and every now and then she was getting a response.

But this particular one was very interesting. It was from Brazil, and they went through a great deal of trouble. To try to let my mother know that there was something hidden in that card!' Ruth couldn't stop laughing.

'Kozienice was famous for its leather business. He mentioned in his letter, that he had a prosperous shoe business in Brazil. He thanked her although it was sad news. He thanked her for everything, and wished her all the best. And that photograph. Well, we remember that.

Now, sometime during this period the two sisters came. They had been with us in the camp. One of the sisters fell fatally ill. I don't remember what her illness was. I also don't remember how the two made it back to Kozienice under these circumstances, but probably the way we did.

It was early March, because by the end of March we buried her. She had been coughing her head off for ten days or maybe for two weeks. She had been there, mostly sleeping. We tried to keep her warm as much as possible.

First Sarah and I burnt down the fence. There had been a picket fence around the house. When we ran out of that wood, we felt that it was our duty to keep the sick girl going. Every now and then we each went out and stole wood.

We didn't exactly get approval from my mother, because she was so honorable, but we didn't get disapproval either. The only thing she said was: 'Remember, these people are trying to keep warm also.'

We never took more than one log from a pile,' Ruth explained. 'They wouldn't miss one log. And we could keep her warm.'

By the end of March, she had died. It was terribly depressing, because it was almost symbolic of all the other deaths,' Ruth said sadly.

'Also, at about the same time,' she continued, 'one night there was banging at the door. I don't remember whether it was two days before she died or whether it was the day of the funeral.

In the middle of the night there was banging on our door, and two men arrived from a small village nearby, where there had been a small Jewish community. A few Jews had returned. I think they said, eight Jews had returned.

That night the Polish inhabitants set fire to the place where they were staying. These men came running barefoot. It was still at the end of winter. Of course, we took them in.

This could have happened in Kozienice too, I suppose. But somehow the Jewish presence had been so large in our town. The Jewish population was almost half. If you counted everything with the suburbs, then it was about thirty percent.'

'How many inhabitants did Kozienice actually have?'

'Before the German occupation, as I understand, there were roughly 20,000 inhabitants of which about 9,000 were Jews. This number swelled to 15,000 as they started to cleanse the countryside of Jews, bringing them into the Kozienice ghetto.

Kozienice had been a prosperous little town, because it had a lot going for it,' Ruth explained to me. 'It had some commerce, some industry, light industry: all the craftsmen, all the shops, many of them shopkeepers, most of them bakers, tailors.

The town had a significant leather industry, because even though it was a cottage industry – small places where eight people were working, ten, twelve people – it was large and important. It employed Polish people too. It didn't just employ Jews.

Kozienice had also tourism because it happened to be in the Lake Country. It had lovely lakes, and there were cottages at the edge of town to rent for the summer at the lake.

It had religious tourism, because of the famous Hassidic dynasty, and the Kozienice rabbi of the 1800s known as the *maggid,* meaning preacher in Hebrew. Jewish pilgrims came to visit his tomb.

The lakes were so close, that our laundress on Mondays used to go down to the lake and rinse the laundry in lake water,' Ruth remembered. 'Somehow it came out better if you gave the last rinse in lake water. You could even wash the linen in lake water. I think village people did, probably not in the wintertime, because the lakes were frozen.

Our laundress and her daughter were washing the laundry in a wooden tub with a scrub board in my Grandma Miriam's laundry room. I remember that clearly. That's where it was washed. Ironically, the daughter of the washerwoman was in the same camp with us, in the same barrack.

I don't remember major anti-Semitic incidents in Kozienice. That doesn't mean it didn't happen, because I lived in my own small world. I was only exposed to people whom my mother let me be exposed to.

The girl had died by the end of March. The funeral was a horrible thing. It was muddy. The snow had just melted,' Ruth told me.

'Somehow, we got a cart and a horse, and we went to the Jewish cemetery. Everybody went, including the three Russian soldiers. When we arrived at the Jewish cemetery the gate still stood, but all else was totally ravished.

We really didn't know where to bury her. There would be a section where her family plot had been, but now every stone was broken, everything was smashed to smithereens. It could not have happened accidentally. It had to be done on purpose.

Everything was so smashed, that even if you put rocks together you could barely figure out a name. But we finally found the spot and could bury her. We said the prayers, and we came back to the house.

The Russian guys had gotten a couple of bottles of vodka. I had never seen anything like this before. Everybody was just sitting around, and whether they had a glass or a cup, it just got filled with vodka, and they drank. Nobody talked.

Everybody was in this trance. I never saw my mother like this. I never saw my mother drink. She was holding a glass that looked like a tea glass. In Poland you drink tea out of glasses. It was half full of that white liquid, with vodka, and my mother drank it.

She was sitting with Sabina. One of the soldiers was sitting next to Sabina. He was the young man who had been from Kozienice. He knew both my mother and Sabina, and the families.

He eventually ended up marrying Sabina, because her husband and her child did not return. He was considerably younger than her, because he ran away as a nineteen-year-old boy. She was already a married woman then with a little child.

I don't know if anyone ever went to sleep. I must have just collapsed, because everybody just sat there.'

'Did you and Sarah get anything to drink?'

'No, we didn't. Sarah and I were just huddling together. We were sitting with the dead girl's sister, the oldest sister, who tried so hard. She was crying a lot.

And that was that!' Ruth gave a deep sigh.

At our next interview Ruth resumed her thoughts about Kozienice: 'Then April came. It was now a week or two after the funeral. All of us were sort of pulling ourselves together. My mother decided, that we were here. And life must go on. Maybe she should try and register me in school. In early April we got up, and she registered me in school. I started in first grade.

Poland had a good school system. There was free public education. Any family who didn't need to put their children to work really early, made sure that their children got at least a few years of education.

My mother had gone to public school, and I would have to go too. After the Germans had moved in it was against the law for Jews to go to a Polish school. While in the ghetto I went to a Jewish school. It was an ad hoc school in a barn where there were two groups; the younger ones were taught by a woman and the older by a man.

I started school. The first few days were confusing and hard, but nothing terribly eventful. There were a couple of girls who were nice to me.

I think at the beginning of the second week, somehow a fight started in the yard. I don't know what it started over, but I know that the boys started throwing stones at us, at the girls.'

'At the Jewish girls?'

'I was the only Jewish girl there was. I was with several other little girls. They started throwing stones. We were ducking. Then they started calling me a dirty Jew. Some of the girls tried to protect me, but some of them got frightened. They ran away and hid. It became a big commotion.

A teacher came out and took care of the fight. Everybody was called in. And my teacher decided, without asking anybody who had started it, that obviously I was the cause of this problem.

Now, I couldn't sit in one of the front rows. I had to sit in the back of the room. I was punished.'

'How unfair!'

'Yeah. When I came home I told my mother. 'What's your teacher's name?' she wanted to know. And I told her what her name was. 'That anti-Semite is still teaching?' my mother cried. 'She gave Chayah a hard time, years ago.'

Chayah was shot during the troubles in the ghetto,' Ruth reminded me. 'She was an orphan, the only child of my mother's second brother. Grandma Miriam raised her as an infant, because her mother died in childbirth, I think I already told you. Her father was still in the military, but later he also died in an epidemic, I think the swine flu, after World War I.

My mother decided it was not an atmosphere where she wanted me to be – after all we had gone through. Being the postmistress, she got all kinds of mail and periodicals concerning Jewish information and Jewish problems from everywhere.

She found out about Joint Distribution, later called American Jewish Joint Distribution, which is still a Jewish charity today. It's a Jewish charity that has existed for more than one hundred years. The reason it's called Joint Distribution is that it's done jointly.

All branches of Judaism, no matter how they argued with each other, would contribute to it. This was like a joint charity for causes that were important to the Jewish community at large.

The headquarters for Joint Distribution at this point were in America. Of course, they weren't in Poland. Joint Distribution had started an orphanage outside of Lodz.

Lodz was the most industrialized city in Poland. All the truly wealthy Jews were living in Lodz. It finally became famous as the center of the textile industry in Poland. Weaving had been a Jewish trade for many generations. When the mechanized weaving came in, the invention, a lot of those weavers were smart enough to start up little companies.

By the time of World War II, they were major factories. Lodz was referred to as the Birmingham of Poland. There were a lot of Jews who owned factories, and they employed hundreds of people.

They had nice lodges at the edge of town. Lodz was not bombed, because the Germans utilized the industry. Lodz was gutted, I would say. All the buildings stood intact: high-rises, full six-story buildings, and more. The streets looked completely intact, windows not broken, or anything.

But the water and the electricity had been shut off. In buildings with elevators, you had to climb stairs. You had to have outhouses in the courtyard, because, even though there were toilets and bathtubs, there was no water. In the outskirts it was different.

The orphanage was a rather nice estate, about half an hour's bus ride outside of Lodz. I am sure the owner of that estate must have had either horse and carriage or maybe even a chauffeured car. It was a very large estate and had been turned into an orphanage. It was entirely supported by Joint Distribution.

That's where my mother wanted me to stay for a while. But the thing was to get me there. It was at the other end of the country. We were in central Poland, and Lodz was in northwestern Poland. Well, my mother and I hitchhiked.'

'Together with Sarah?'

'No, Sarah actually stayed behind, because my mother had the obligation of being the postmistress. Somebody had to be there. Sarah stayed behind with Sabina, and they were taking care of that.

Before I continue with our trip to Lodz,' Ruth told me when we met again, 'I should tell you what happened to the family pictures you've been looking at.

It was sometime after we had buried the girl. The snow had melted. Then my mother decided that we finally go over to the former ghetto where my grandparents' house used to be. Now that the snow had totally melted we could see the completely ruined former ghetto. I remember that among rubble and rocks I saw a skeleton of a house and half a chimney.

My mother started to measure the distance from the town's major fountain towards the former ghetto. The fountain also was partially ruined, but you could recognize where it had been. It had been a fountain that was fed by spring water. There was no running water now.

As we continued walking we saw some goats grazing.

'It is now 200 meters from the fountain,' my mother explained. We were standing on a sidewalk that was sort of intact. She climbed up on some rubble and was looking whether she could find anything. And then she decided: 'This is where our house stood. It was 200 meters from the fountain.'

While Sarah and I were watching the skinny goats grazing peacefully on the grass that had sprung up amidst the rubble and ruins, a man came out of nowhere it seemed. 'These are my goats,' he said coming towards us. He must have assumed we were out to steal his goats.

My mother went over to him and looked him straight in the eyes. 'They may be your goats but they are grazing on my property. This is my land,' she said. 'By all rights, I should charge you rent for your goats grazing here.' After they had talked for a while they agreed that whatever the goats would dig up belonged to my mother.

She knew that my grandparents had buried a lot in the backyard when the Germans had moved into town – like their silverware; the breastplates with Hebrew inscription and silver for twelve, which my grandmother used for *Seder*; rare books; and a lot of other valuable things.

But the only thing the man came up with were partially chewed photographs by his goats. He had kept them in a shoebox. That's why our photos were in such bad shape,' Ruth explained.

'Sarah being artistic, glued the pieces on stationery leaving space empty for other pieces to glue together – like in a puzzle. Later in Sweden a photographer dealt with them first. And in New York my friend Miriam, who is a professional artist, gave the last touch to these pictures as you can see them now here on my kitchen table.

Anyway, my mother went back the next day. She told the man that she knew that there were more things buried in her mother's backyard. 'Perhaps you took them,' she said firmly, 'or the Germans or whoever. But I should at least have some money for them.'

He probably didn't have much money himself, but he gave her enough so she could buy a small suitcase, definitely used, and some decent clothes: a dress, a jacket, and a hat. And that's what she got for the ravaged home.'

'It's quite amazing, Ruth. But I hardly noticed that your pictures were partially damaged. I guess, I was just happy you had some photos of your family.'

'Let's go back now to our trip to Lodz,' Ruth went on. 'My mother and I were travelling on Russian trucks, on military trucks. It took us quite a few days but we finally got there. The thing that I remember most from that journey was traversing Warsaw. Going directly up north, the major road from Kozienice went straight to Warsaw, as the crow flies, my mother had pointed out.

You are not talking about twisty roads or anything. Straight from Kozienice to Warsaw is about fifty-eight kilometers. The most common route was going up the Vistula. There were regular ferries.

We were hitchhiking. Traversing Warsaw was the eeriest thing. There was not one building intact. There was one road that had been cleared. Some military vehicles were going through it, and the rubble was on all sides.

When I looked up from the back of the truck we were in I could see that there were two stories of a house that had been an eight-story building. There were people living there. The rest was rubble. All we saw was just rubble, as far as the eye could see.

That was my first sight of Warsaw. Even though I had been born there, I left when I was six weeks old,' Ruth reminded me. 'The next time I saw Warsaw again, was the summer of my husband's concert tour. And then I went to all the restored places.'

9

Lodz

'Finally, we got to the orphanage outside of Lodz, and my mother made some arrangements. She signed me up. They were just collecting children hidden by peasants, whom they found. And children who had somehow wandered off and had survived on their own.

They preferred young teenagers, because they had this deal, that if they got them healthy and in good physical shape, they would transport them to Cyprus.'

'Why did they do that, Ruth?'

'They wanted Jews to return to Palestine.

The British were running Palestine. The Arabs didn't want Jews to come. The British were accommodating the Arabs, even though Jews didn't have any place else to go. There was only a small Jewish community from pre-war. That community wanted Jews to come. But they had to do it surreptitiously.

You went to Cyprus. Cyprus was close enough, so that at night you went on rowboats and you were smuggled into Palestine. There was no Israel then. It was Palestine. Every now and then the British would catch a boat and send it back to Cyprus. But they didn't shoot.'

'But you stayed with your mother?'

'Yes. I am telling you this, because my mother found out that that's what they were doing with most of the older children. The little ones they couldn't transport.

My mother decided: 'Absolutely, don't ship her anywhere. I am doing this out of desperation, because I can't keep my daughter where I am. I have neither medical care for her, nor education, nor anything. I will come back and get her as soon as I find work and a place to live.'

They promised.

My mother was already making plans to leave Kozienice, without my knowing it,' Ruth told me. 'I don't remember too much about the orphanage, because I was thrown together with approximately sixty to eighty children. The number always varied. There were always children coming and children leaving.

I never had been vaccinated. None of us had been vaccinated because of the war. We were giving each other everything. The only thing in this place that was thriving was the infirmary. It was a separate building. They had several Jewish women physicians, who had been physicians before the war.

I got measles. I got mumps. I got chicken pox. It seemed as soon as I got out of the infirmary and was back in my bed, three days later I would return to the infirmary.' Ruth had a good laugh, remembering this.

'That was my story,' she said.

'There is that beautiful picture from the orphanage,' I pointed out to Ruth. 'You all are eating soup with huge silver spoons.'

'Yeah, they were utilizing everything from that estate. It was a lovely estate with beautiful rooms. The rooms were so big that they had ten cots in each room. Former schoolteachers were taking care of us.

The rules in this orphanage were quite interesting. At night you got undressed and you'd put all your clothes on one pile on the floor. You put on a nightdress. You had a mug, but it wasn't a porcelain one; it was like these pots here.' Ruth pointed to one of her pots on the kitchen stove.

'It was metal with enamel inside. You had a mug, a toothbrush, and a towel. There was a shelf above the cot where you kept the mug and the toothbrush. In the morning when you got up there was a pile of clean clothes. You put on whatever fit you, because none of us had her own clothes.

I was the smallest one. The big girls always got first pick and they pushed me away,' Ruth said laughing.

'They couldn't fit into your size anyway.'

'That's right. I always ended up with what was left. I would say, eight times out of ten I was wearing boys' clothes, because that's what was left.

And look, I didn't really know the difference. But in retrospect, I was wearing these riding breeches. Those were definitely boys' pants. They were riding pants. With snaps on the side,' Ruth said amused. 'I often ended up with those.

But there was one thing I always got. Some little girl in America had gotten black and white patent leather shoes for a party. Later her mother must have given them away for the poor people. They didn't fit anybody. They only fit me. I always had my black and white patent leather shoes. It didn't matter what weather it was. They were my shoes. They fit me and not anybody else.'

'Now, let's see. You stayed in the orphanage, and your mother went back to Kozienice and packed up, right?'

'Yes, she promised me that she would come soon and get me. If I wasn't sick, I would take myself to the road and look for my mother. Nothing could drag me away except for the meal.

Finally, I got a visitor. Sabina came. I had been there for two or two and half months. It seemed the longest period of my life, because this was the only time I was without my mother,' Ruth almost whispered.

'I missed her so much. I didn't know where my mother was. I didn't know where Sarah was. Kozienice could have been at the other end of the world,' Ruth said.

I didn't go to school much, because I was sick most of the time. I didn't benefit from that. But the summer was fairly nice being outside. There were lots of flower gardens that had been neglected, but they were so pretty.

Sabina came in May, I remember, because the tulips came out. She said, she had already left and Mama was finishing up things. She was going to come soon. I shouldn't worry. She was making some arrangements to come to Lodz.

Much later – we were already living in New York – my mother told me that she had gotten a letter from a man, who was not exactly from our town but from our region. He had been in Buchenwald with my father. My father had gone through several camps before.

As the war proceeded the Allies' bombing of Germany intensified and this included trains that might be carrying ammunition and weapons,' Ruth explained.

'The Buchenwald authorities might have believed that the Allies were more interested in the trains than in the camp, and therefore imprisoned inmates in trains. There was a siding not far from Buchenwald.[1]

My father was on one of these trains. It was hit during the liberation of Buchenwald at the beginning of April 1945 by US forces.'

Ruth fell silent. She seemed so fragile and sad. After a while she continued.

'My mother really didn't want to talk about that letter. I never got details. It took some time before I ever became aware that the letter existed.

The prisoners in the car shared their last names and the towns where they lived. They promised each other that if any of them survived, they would notify the family. They memorized the hometowns and the last names. Never mind addresses, just Jewish community.

This man happened to be from a nearby town. He wrote that there were a few of them still alive, including him, when the Allies broke the train car open. Most of them had died from their wounds or suffocated. Of the few they got to a hospital, he was the one who survived. He was now spending his time writing the letters to those he could remember.

That's all I know about my father,' Ruth said, trying to control her feelings.

'He was taken away together with uncle Maier. They soon were separated. Maier must have died in Auschwitz. Father was physically stronger than Maier. That's how it seemed to me as a little girl. My father had broad shoulders. He was muscular. If anyone should have survived my father was the one.'

'It's all very, very sad, Ruth.'

This day, while listening to Ruth telling me about the death of her father; sensing her sadness, especially as she was so distant from his death, I thought of my own father's fate.

****

My mother got his last news at the beginning of April 1945. My father was on the way to Gotha, a town only about 50 kilometers from Weimar-Buchenwald.

Only a few days before, on his last short visit to Hödingen at the end of March, he had revealed to my mother that if he stole a suit from a civilian, they probably would shoot him.

Later, three days before the end of the war, my mother's cousin heard on the radio in Lörrach, that my father and others, because of 'cowardice in front of the enemy,' were to be executed that day by hanging. My mother had told me much later.

How did my father without any marching orders make his way down to this little southern town, where his sons were born? I asked myself.

After the fall of the Berlin Wall I went in search of my father, traveling with my husband from New York to Gotha. Gotha, like Weimar, is a town in Germany that became part of the former GDR.

Toward the end of the war my father had sent his last sign of life from this town: 'We will have to leave any hour,' he wrote, 'to where we don't know.'

My mother had told me that our father probably had deserted. Since there was no word from him she assumed he was dead. After the war she declared him dead. She needed the war widows' pension to survive with her three children. Until her own death she paid grave care in Gotha where my father supposedly lay buried.

We found a stone cross with his name and the names of five other soldiers in the *Hauptfriedhof* Gotha, in the military cemetery. It stood in the shadow of a cypress at the far end of the cemetery.

My husband came over to me and asked: 'Is this where your father lies buried?' 'His name is engraved on this cross,' I said. He put his arm around my shoulder and we stood by my father's grave in silence. But I didn't really believe that my father lay buried there. Yet I couldn't stop my tears.

✳✳✳✳

Ruth and I, that day on our walk back to the railroad station, went in silence. Ruth had taken my arm. And when the train to New York was approaching the station, we both hugged each other, saying good-bye.

The next time we met only briefly. Ruth told me again that because her mother was the town's Jewish postmistress she had received that letter. Now she could finally leave Kozienice. There was no more reason to stay.

'She applied for a passport, because Ruczka was able to send papers that she would sponsor us to come to America. For that we needed all the legal documents. And, of course, we needed a passport. It took my mother quite a long time to gather all of this. She would accept a transit visa to any country just to get out of Poland. 'I survived Hitler. I don't have the energy to survive Stalin,' she explained.

My mother was born and went to school in Kozienice. Some records were in disarray but the school records were all there. But she was married in Radom.

Now, the reason for this was that grandpa Leib's business already at that time wasn't thriving too well anymore. He was selling blacksmiths' supplies, as you remember. His clients were from the countryside.

Only on market day, on Wednesdays, his shop was open. It was open from dawn to dusk. On other days people had to ring a bell, and then grandpa or grandma would open the door. The bell rang in the back of the house in their apartment. I told you that before.

Anyway, in this position – before his business had been a thriving business – he could not afford to give a proper Orthodox wedding for his youngest daughter. In his former position he would have invited the whole community, and the beggars as well. For them a separate long table was provided. The Yiddish saying, that a poor man eats well when a rich man marries off his daughter, probably didn't apply this time.

The decision was to have the wedding at one of mother's numerous siblings, at her sister Matel's house in Radom. Her husband had a tannery, and they were well off.

One of grandpa's nieces, also a Luksenburg, was married to a rabbi. He performed the ceremony in his study. The celebration took place in Matel's house. It was a 'modest' wedding. About sixty to eighty relatives had been invited.

There was, of course, no marriage certificate of my parents on file in the town hall of Kozience. Since my mother now wanted to get out of Poland as fast as possible, because she didn't believe that Stalin would move out soon in the future, she was pushing for a passport.

'You know me,' my mother insisted. 'I was born here,' she told the town hall officials. 'I went to school here. I'm a Luksenburg.'

'Of course, we know the Luksenburgs,' they admitted. 'We remember your husband, *Pan* Motek, the Luksenburg son-in-law, as they would refer to him. The Luksenburgs had been around in Kozienice for several generations.'

'Why don't we give you a passport in your maiden name?' they suggested.

And they did. They gave her a passport in her maiden name with me, the child Ruth Luksenburg, mentioned in it.

This is how I lost my last name Kalb,' Ruth explained. She proudly showed me an old passport, issued in Warsaw, with all the stamps for the years of her Swedish exile.

We continued at our next interview, with Ruth's anxious waiting for her mother to come to Lodz.

'Sabina at that time knew already that my mother had been contacted to run a soup kitchen in Lodz.'

'Through the same organization?'

'No, this was through a completely different organization: a Jewish labor organization in the United States that was trying to be helpful – to feed the hungry Jews in Poland.

They thought if they couldn't do anything legally, maybe they could do it illegally. They would send funds; and someone could start a soup kitchen, buy food on the black market, and feed the people.

The Jewish Labor Committee . . . Of course, Ruczka, my cousin Rose Luksenburg, Rose Alexander by that point, went to tell them that her aunt, Pola Luksenburg, was in Poland and she should be a candidate for this position.

That Committee checked out my mother's pre-war credentials. They checked her out, probably through Jewish labor union leaders who had since come to the United States. Long before the war Pola had been an active member of the Jewish Labor Bund in Poland, a socialist organization. She always had been an activist for the downtrodden.

You remember that she taught, at twelve years old, the Jewish boys in Kozienice to read Polish, so they could ask for better pay?'

'Yes, I remember.'

'My mother actually met my father in the Socialist Youth Movement *Die Jugend* in Przemysl. At that time, she was helping her brother Daniel in his shop. My parents, already at a young age, shared socialist ideas and values.

Well, my mother came to Lodz and she now had this position. You see, Stalin was going to start releasing the Jews who had escaped to Russia. The Committee must have figured that there was semi-starvation in Poland already. If you were going to get thousands of people who were trying to get back from Russia it was going to be horrific.

My mother's job was to start a soup kitchen. They would provide her with funds. She had to find the location, a place that would fit about three hundred people at a sitting. She found a location. She got seven women she knew as very hard working from the previous camps who happened to be in Lodz. Four worked in the kitchen. The others helped my mother getting food and carrying it.

She couldn't get a ground floor. She didn't have enough money. But she got one, one flight up. She got a room for herself and Sarah. And then my mother came and got me,' Ruth quietly said.

'How good, Ruth.' I grabbed her hand. I knew she was very moved.

'Yeah,' Ruth said. She gave a deep sigh. But then she went on: 'My mother was going together with her helpers to the countryside. She paid the peasants with dollars to give her barley, potatoes, carrots, cabbage.

The women were cooking for three feedings. Three feedings – but the problem was water! It was a nice big kitchen. It was the equivalent of a six-room apartment that she had found.

In the big rooms she had opened the sliding doors between what had been the parlor and the dining room. But no water. Water had to be fetched from a water dispensing station. You stood with two buckets on line, and they filled them up.

Sarah and I became the water carriers,' Ruth remembered proudly. 'We would start at the crack of dawn, because the women already were preparing for cooking. We got on line and waited.

I remember I would always spill a lot of the water going upstairs,' Ruth told me laughing. 'Because I was so little! It was hard. And then we delivered the water.

'We're glad you're here,' the women would say. 'Now we can start.' They were peeling potatoes. They were always peeling potatoes. They could start cooking. Any water like from draining something was stored in the bathtub. It was a large bathroom.

It was stored there, because then you could use that water for washing the dishes. That water was also for rinsing the peeled potatoes or vegetables. Afterwards you put that water in buckets and you mopped the floor. Water was such a major problem.

When Sarah and I brought the last load of buckets, the women would invite us to eat: 'Soup's ready, girls. Sit down.'

And we would sit down and eat our nice fresh soup to our heart's content, before they opened the doors and let the first bunch of people in. There was always a long line. There was always a line, especially when Stalin gave the Jews only two weeks to leave. You have two weeks to leave or you will stay in Russia, he had declared or something like that, as I remember.

People were coming like crazy. We were getting hundreds. We were getting thousands. People were hanging onto doors travelling on trains. They were on the roofs of trains. That's when Oscar's family also fled Russia.

That would be a story between us, because that has nothing to do with us. I am only mentioning it, because they came through Lodz while my mother was running the soup kitchen.'

'That's amazing.'

'We didn't meet. But they were aware of the soup kitchen. They had taken advantage of the soup kitchen during the brief time they were in Lodz.' Ruth had a big laugh.

'You and Oscar had to wait to meet in America,' I exclaimed.

'Many years later at a fundraiser in America,' Ruth exclaimed. 'We didn't meet in Lodz. But I know that they had gone through Lodz, and that Oscar's family had partaken of the soup kitchen. Later in New York my mother-in-law asked me: 'Was your mother running that soup kitchen in Lodz?'

They actually had, when they were desperate enough, got on line one day for the soup kitchen,' she said.

'That's fantastic. Your future husband was already in the picture as a little boy.

Now, do you want to talk about the next stage of your exodus from Poland to America, Ruth? Or do you want to say more about Lodz?'

'Basically, it was hard in Lodz, but we were together, that part of us that was alive. My mother was getting regular letters from her niece Ruczka, who had gotten to New York.

Now in New York, Ruczka was a registered nurse and they needed nurses. There were Jewish tenements and a visiting nurse, a nurse who spoke Yiddish . . .!' Ruth exclaimed.

'They had those old Jews who had gotten left behind in the tenements, the walk-ups. They needed nurse service, and she was hired immediately.'

'Ruczka is the one who got you over.'

'Yes, she was the daughter of my mother's older brother Yechel. Do you remember? He had a daughter and a son. And the daughter was Rose, or Ruczka, and the son was Daniel. My cousin survived because she came with her husband to New York. She was grabbed up. She got work instantly. She was working for the Visiting Nurse Service.'

Ruth pointed at a picture on the kitchen table. 'This was when Ruczka came to Kozienice. My grandma Toba, after visiting me for the first time, left Kozienice before the Germans came, as you remember. Ruczka came, because she wanted to say good-bye. She had spent every summer growing up being sent to grandma Miriam's house for the summer. Especially since she was a half-orphan.

Her father had died in one of the epidemics in World War I. It was swine flu or something like that, I already told you. It was some kind of terrible flu.

My grandmother was so proud. She had nine children. She raised nine children. But, poor grandma, she lost two sons within the same year. Of course, she never found out that only my mother survived of all her children.

I have another picture of Ruczka when she graduated from Columbia University in New York. At that time, the word was from the Polish government in exile, that preparations were being made for people to go back and help rebuild Poland after the war.

This was the Polish government in exile, of course. They were willing to help train people who would be able to rebuild the country. Ruczka was right there on line and she was already a nurse. They decided to send her to Columbia University's School of Public Health. And she got her degree in social work.

She was a godsend. She was the one who adopted Sarah. She was the one who brought us over here too.'

'Let's go on from here, Ruth. Why don't you talk about what happened after Lodz? I think your next destination was Sweden. Why don't you talk about Sweden?'

But Ruth switched back to Lodz once more: 'My mother was working in the soup kitchen in Lodz. We were all three sleeping in one room. Sarah and I shared a bed, and my mother slept on the couch. It was a walk-up.

There was no electricity. It was a lovely apartment building. The one room we were staying in was obviously a bedroom. But we were the three of us. And there were other people in other rooms.

There was a lovely bathroom and a lovely kitchen, but no running water and no electricity. We used candles or kerosene lamps. Whatever you could get your hands on. And there were now trees in the courtyard where there had been fountains or a flower garden. It was actually disgusting, because what had once been a nicely landscaped flower garden was now where the outhouses stood. All the apartments were full of people. The outhouses were not taken care of. It stank. This was not great living. We were eating in the soup kitchen. And we started out early; Sarah and I carrying water.'

'You couldn't go to school?'

'Of course not. In every spare moment my mother went from embassy to embassy explaining: 'I have papers for America. All I need is a short transit visa for your country.'

My mother's ears were tuned into the fact that Stalin was making himself terribly comfortable in Poland. It didn't look like he was going to leave. 'I survived Hitler. I don't have the energy to survive Stalin,' became her mantra.

That's what she kept repeating to us. Because we kept asking her: 'Mama, why don't you relax? Why do you always keep running when you are not working?' Because when she was working she was in the countryside scrounging for vegetables, potatoes, and onions. Everything had to be done on foot. Nothing worked. No transportation.'

'But she had helpers to carry it?'

'Yeah. But we continued asking her: 'Why don't you just rest?' 'I got to find a place to go,' she would say.

After having been told 'no' from almost every major country she had tried, finally Sweden said: 'OK, three months.' And my mother cried: 'Wonderful! Three months.'

The American immigration system is lousy now and was even lousier then, I think. If you had a sibling or a spouse you could come very quickly. But the more distant the relationship, you were put on a waiting list.'

'You only had Ruczka.'

'Right, Ruczka my cousin, and my mother's niece. They are distant relatives. She knew it. But Sweden wasn't going to deport her, was more likely going to extend the visa, she thought. She was taking a chance.

My mother immediately sent a telegram to Ruczka telling her that we were offered a transit visa. My cousin was so happy. She borrowed money from her employer so that we could buy a ticket. We would go by boat from the Polish port on the Baltic Sea to Sweden.

She sent us money. I don't remember how quickly it came. But as soon as that was possible I think we went by train to Gdynia. From there we took a boat to Sweden. The boat was called *Trelleborg*. It shows in my mother's passport.'

Ruth showed me on the map. 'Here it is: Gdansk and Gdynia. Well, it's the bay of Gdansk. Gdynia is the active port and you take an overnight boat to Sweden. That's all I remember.'

Note

1. 'A rail siding completed in 1943 connected the camp with the freight yards in Weimar, facilitating the shipment of war supplies' (Holocaust Encyclopedia, United States Holocaust Memorial Museum).

Reference

United States Holocaust Memorial Museum. 'Buchenwald.' Holocaust Encyclopedia. www.ushmm.org/wlc/en/article.php?ModuleId=10005143. Accessed on 3 March 2016.

10

Sweden

'How long after the war did you arrive in Sweden, Ruth?' I asked at our next meeting.

'We arrived in Göteborg on March 28, 1946. Ruczka had gotten in touch with the Jewish community in Sweden. She had arranged housing for us. She wrote to all kinds of committees.

She got in touch with the Jewish Socialists in Sweden. That's what she was looking for, because they would have some kind of connection with her and her late husband.

There was a small group of Jews in Sweden. I surmise they had come to Sweden after the First Russian Revolution in 1905 or even before; during the pogroms in the 1860s and 1870s when there was continuous trouble for Jews of Russian descent.

One of them was Mr. Olberg, a white haired, distinguished gentleman. He had been born in Russia and had spent the last forty years in Sweden. He was well established in Sweden.

Mr. Olberg met us at the harbor and took us by train to Stockholm. He set us up in the suburbs of Stockholm where there were other Jewish families. I loosely call them families. In some instances, there was a husband and wife, in some instances there was a mother and a daughter. The largest unit was actually three.

It was an old *Pension* at the outskirts of Stockholm. In the summer it was still utilized. But since it was off-season, they rented it very cheaply.

We were all using the community kitchen, because it had been a *Pension*. There was one bathroom, and there was a chart on the wall when you were allowed to use the bathroom. There was one extra toilet on each floor. The bathroom had a tub, a hand-held shower and a sink. All of us were to keep a pitcher of water with a little bowl in our rooms, so we could throw some water on our face in the morning.

We ended up thirteen family units all squeezed in the same house. There was one room to a family, no matter how big the family was. That's where we were.

Eventually another Jewish lady, Mrs. Meer, who was a friend of the gentleman of this group, came to visit us. She was so well established that her son was already in Parliament. He was a member of the Swedish Parliament. I eventually became kind of friendly with her granddaughter. She brought her granddaughter along a few times.

We arrived on the 28th of March 46. After some time, my mother decided she should register me for school.'

'You didn't speak a word of Swedish!'

'Of course not! My mother spoke German to the principal whose German was impeccable. She told my mother that her parents had come from Russia after the First Revolution. She and her siblings were educated in Sweden.

Even though I was nine years old, perhaps the best thing to do was to put me in the first grade. It was late spring and I could learn Swedish at my own pace. And in the fall, I could be in second grade. I had to learn everything. I had basically not been to school by this point.

The next morning, I packed a paper bag with a sandwich and went off to school. I only just had been registered. My mother had taken me over towards the end of the previous day. 'This is where you are going to, this is the door,' she had explained to me.

Actually, I shook hands with the first-grade teacher. My mother said something to her, and I would be starting tomorrow. It was going to be fine. It was all hunky-dory. I would go tomorrow and I would have my first day of school. But in fact, I was so confused. I didn't know what was going on.

I think I must have had two days of school, because on the third day I was approaching school with my sandwich bag and I saw something very strange. There were trucks in front of the school. My antenna went up.

Yes, trucks. There were trucks. I got a little closer and I thought: These stupid kids are so happy running up on the steps of these trucks!' Ruth almost screamed in disbelief.

'It was like campers, and there were two steps and benches on each side. What idiots these kids are. I turned on my heels and I took off. I ran back home like crazy.

My mother was in such a shock. She wasn't working yet. She was home. I couldn't catch my breath. I was panting. My mother cried: 'What happened?'

'They're doing it here too! They're doing it here too!' I screamed. And all she could get out of me was: 'They're doing it here too!'

I wanted to hide.' Ruth was now laughing. 'I was looking for a hiding place. My mother was trying to communicate with me. Well, she finally got something out of me.

It was a day before the first of May. There was some kind of outing for the children. Nobody told me,' Ruth exclaimed.

'The next day was actually the first of May and it was a holiday. No school. My mother took Sarah and me on the bus to the city of Stockholm. We went to the park to see what the first of May was like.

Because my mother couldn't calm me down. She had gone to school and talked to the principal. She found out that it was an outing just for the children.

She took us and we went to the park. There were events, parades, and festivities. Everyone was very happy. People were singing and dancing.

My mother did a wonderful thing for me.' Ruth was speaking softly now, still remembering that incident.

'You see that man there, selling something?' my mother asked me. 'That's something you've never had. But it's wonderful.'

She took out whatever little Swedish money she had, because Mr. Olberg had given us pocket money. She got me a vanilla ice cream cone. My first ever ice cream.'

'That surely must have soothed you.'

'My eyes almost popped out of my head. I never had anything like that,' Ruth whispered. 'I could see Sarah how she looked at my ice cream cone. She had it in Warsaw, of course. She knew what that was. But my mother didn't have money for two. And I needed the soothing.

'You start,' my mother said to me. 'But then you must share with Sarah.' Of course, I would. We both always shared everything.

Every year my mother would take us to the park in Stockholm to watch the May Day celebrations. In addition to the enormous impression these celebrations made on me, I also remember when I saw and heard for the first time Paul Robeson, the famous civil rights activist and singer.

He came to Sweden to sing on May Day one year. I don't remember which year; perhaps it was in 1949, the year when we left Sweden for Canada.

I remember that we heard singing in the distance. We were walking towards that. There was a mass of people, hundreds, maybe even thousands, I thought, though Stockholm wasn't such a populated city.

In the distance there was a stage, like a band shell stage. There was that gorgeous voice coming from there, an unbelievable voice. And as we got closer, I saw a man – a very large man. I figured there was a giant with a gigantic voice. But there was something more that I couldn't fathom. The man was pitch black. It was Paul Robeson.'

Ruth told me, that she would never forget his voice, this wonderful voice that sang of the deep American South and the sufferings of his people.

'That's how things were for me then,' Ruth continued. 'It was decided since there were only a few weeks left of school, it might be wiser for me to become accustomed to the sound of the language, to being there, and start school in the fall when everybody else was starting school.

It made perfect sense to wait with school, also because of my bad health, which was among other things the result of severe starvation in the camps. My mother now was feeding me good nutritious food, but I couldn't digest it. The minute I ate it, I threw up.

She took me to a children's hospital in Stockholm. That's when the pediatrician insisted that I was three, but I was really nine. Maybe his German wasn't good enough or my mother thought maybe her German wasn't good enough, so they started writing to each other.

He wrote three and said: '*drei*.' And my mother crossed it out and wrote nine and said: '*neun*.' Finally, he gave up, because he figured if I was nine, they better take me in and check me out thoroughly,' Ruth explained.

'I spent a week, maybe ten days in the hospital. And they really checked me thoroughly. Well, I had been sick a lot. But being sick in the camps didn't really count as being sick.

I wasn't really sick. I was just miserable all the time. Sometimes in the camps, my mother would touch my forehead to see if I was running a fever. But even if I had a fever there was nothing one could do about it.

In the hospital they found out that my baby teeth were all rotten. They all had to be removed. The first thing they noticed, I was swallowing pus with every mouthful of food. That couldn't be good. Anyway, I was sort of doctored up.

First, they gave me injections of vitamins. And then they gave my mother a bottle of vitamins, especially the B12s for growth, to get me going. I had an enormous growing spurt that year. Actually, I think I got to the size I am now within two years in Sweden.'

'In the picture that shows you in the Swedish countryside, you look already like a big girl.'

'Yes, a big girl. My mother was stuffing me with food. She wanted all those good things for me: berries with cream and all. We went out and picked berries right behind our house. We picked blueberries by the bushel. She was cooking these delicious foods for all of us, because everybody was emaciated.

She took us to the woods, and we learned how to pick sorrel, which are those green leaves that make a wonderful soup. We picked all the berries. We picked blueberries and blackberries.'

'And strawberries?'

'Not there. But when we were later living in the manor house. In the back of that house was an abandoned orchard. We picked the plums, and my mother made jam out of them. There were also these little green berries. I never saw them in the United States.'

'Oh, gooseberries!'

'Gooseberries! Lots and lots of gooseberries! We used to get packages of sugar from the United States. Ruczka sent us sugar. My mother made jam out of those gooseberries.'

****

I remembered, that at about the same time, my mother, my two brothers, and I picked berries in the forest around Hödingen. We would leave early in the morning. I, the youngest, just watched them pick blueberries or raspberries. Or I played with my dog, a little mutt I got for my birthday.

Around midday usually the bucket would be filled. That was the moment my mother handed out to each of us a sandwich made of delicious sourdough rye bread she used to buy from the baker in the village.

Later when we got back home my mother reminded my brothers to watch over their little sister, and already we could see her leaving on my father's old bicycle riding down the village road. She was going to exchange the fresh berries for some fat, or even some sausages, in a hospital in the nearest western town, Helmstedt.

Hödingen, a village in the eastern sector, was only twenty-four kilometers away from that border town; Germany being divided into west and east after its defeat in the Second World War.

My mother also smuggled people for money over the border, in order to buy food in the West. My aunt from Berlin would come to stay with us children.

It was extremely dangerous for our mother. People got killed for a bag of food, particularly in the dark of the forest she had to cross. I remember the fear that gripped us. We would watch out for her late in the evening, standing at the kitchen window; looking down the dark village road; praying for our mother to come back.

****

'Resourcefulness under any circumstances,' Ruth said with enthusiasm. 'My mother was never trained to be a seamstress. But she sewed her own trousseau. She knew how to sew. She did alterations in exchange for English lessons.

My mother was, as far as I'm concerned, superhuman. She was a super woman,' Ruth proudly declared. 'For me she was the tiniest, tiniest super woman in the world, because she was stuck with two children for the entire war.

I remember my mother saying that when they started taking people for slave labor, the Germans decided that anyone fifteen years and older would be considered able-bodied. As I have mentioned before, Sarah was too young to be considered able-bodied. She was born in the fall of 1929. She was tall for her age. Therefore, she had to lie about her age. All her documents were in Warsaw.'

'I started eating well,' Ruth continued at our next meeting. 'By the end of that summer I was already growing and gaining strength. Our house was near the water. I was in the water every day.

The first place we stayed was called Saltsjöbaden. We didn't stay in Saltsjöbaden directly, because that was a fancy area. We stayed two towns away, in a smaller place called Neglingeon. We stayed in a fairly run-down *Pension*. We lived there. But then the committee decided that even that was too expensive, because it got into the summer.'

'The committee paid for it?'

'Yes, because we didn't have anything. They had to. Well, we only came in contact with Mr. Olberg and Mrs. Meer. But it was a larger committee from what I understand. These two people decided it was too expensive and they were looking for a less expensive place.

They found an abandoned manor house for all of us, as I mentioned earlier. It was at the end of a road. The building was about three hundred years old. It had been unoccupied for a while. But it had central heating and a coal stove for cooking.

It was big enough because it had been a manor house. It had servant's quarters, whatever, but it was old and run-down. On both sides of the road that led to the bus stop, there were modern homes owned by Swedish families. And the road ended at our house.

I have a picture of it. I will show you. Behind there were gardens and a sort of run-down orchard. There was a lake. I could swim. The place had a rowboat. I could drag it down and would go out rowing. It was a very nice summer. And then I started school.

Ruth in the summer camp in Neglingeon, Sweden in August 1946 (Ruth on the left)

Now I was a real person, not an animal that had been hiding for years. I didn't eat with my hands anymore. I used a spoon and a fork. My mother had the patience and time to teach me how to hold a knife. All these things you don't even think of were happening during this summer.'

'In the summer of 46?'

'That's right, in the summer of 46. When I started school that year in the fall, I was also not the only Jewish child that was starting school, because there was a woman who came with her daughter, Maryla, who was added to our complex.

It wasn't actually her daughter. She had found her sister's daughter after the war. She came to Sweden either through her husband, whom she had lost or through her sister's family, who also had some connection with the socialists in Poland. They got in touch with the same people who brought us there.'

'Now you had a friend, Ruth.'

'Yes, Maryla was more or less my age and she had been hidden in different ways. She lost both parents. She was with her aunt. There was another aunt in Australia. They were aiming for Australia. They left Sweden much earlier. But I had her as a friend for a while.'

'Did you slowly manage with Swedish?'

'Yes, remember I was tri-lingual already. I was even more than tri-lingual, because I immediately picked up Russian. I lived under Russian occupation for a little over a year, from January 45 to March 46.

So Russian was all right. Like German had been all right. It was in the street, on the trucks when we hitchhiked to the orphanage. They were Russian soldiers. The short time we were in Kozienice, there were Russian soldiers in the street.

Well, there were four languages in my head already. The more languages you know, the easier it is to learn another. I was picking up Swedish. Some of the words are like German and, of course, the neighbors in the houses on the road all had children who spoke Swedish. They tried to talk to us.

One day a little girl actually took me by the hand, took me to the back of the house. It was the family's summer cottage. I know that, because she disappeared in the fall. In the back of the summer cottage there was a little house. It was a dollhouse. Her father had built it. It had a little door and there were dolls inside.'

'She explained all that to you in Swedish?'

'Yes, she was going on in Swedish, and I was trying to figure out what she was telling me. But after doing these things, being down at the lake with her, being with the dolls – I could manage.

It was challenging, because I was little. It wasn't even embarrassing, because I was small like most of their first graders. And I fit in. Except for little things like one involving a schoolmate Jan who sat across from me.

One day he came to school and asked me: 'Rut' – that's how you pronounce my name in Swedish – 'Rut can I touch your hair?'

'Yeah, I said.' I figured he never had seen dark curly hair. Everyone in the class was blond and blue-eyed. It looked like their hair had faded in the sun during the summer. He was touching my hair.

'What's wrong?' I asked him. 'I can't find them,' he said. I didn't know what he was looking for.

He had told his parents at home that there was a Jewish girl in school. And what was Jewish? His parents opened an art book and showed him a picture of a sculpture of Moses. Moses had, as he told me, little horns. It was a picture of the sculpture of Moses by the famous Michelangelo.

Moses had met God on Mount Sinai. He was given the Ten Commandments,' Ruth explained to me. 'Even today in an Orthodox synagogue, Moses descending from Mount Sinai, is described as having a glow around his head. It is based on the ancient Hebrew text.

The misinterpretation of this glow as horns included all Jews, even as late as 1946 in Sweden,' Ruth said, annoyed.

'And six million of your people died because of such prejudice,' I added. 'Can we ever eradicate prejudice, Ruth? Will it ever end?'

Ruth told me about a priest who would come to school, when we met again. 'Sweden was a Lutheran country and very strict. He would teach religion. I think it was once a week for an afternoon. But maybe it was just for an hour. It was always after lunch.

I inherited stubbornness from my mother, I guess. I didn't want to be part of the class. I told him, probably in very broken Swedish, that I didn't need another religion, that I already had one. Although, as I told you, I never was devoutly religious.

He told me, he knew. But it was a course, and I was expected to take part in the course. It was a tug of war through the whole year.

I told him I didn't want to take part in the class. During the course, could I sit in the back of the room? And I would take the exam. We finally settled on that.

Twice a year there were outings to a church, for the whole school. I did that. I couldn't come up with any reason why not. It was part of the course and there were excursions for the course.

But I tell you, with a full church, the kids and adults kneeling, and me standing at attention – that was my thing. I stood at attention forever,' Ruth said proudly.

'But he never said anything, and I always passed the course.

Otherwise I made friends, I spoke Swedish, and learned how to ride a bicycle, because the school was far. My mother bought me a bicycle for my eleventh birthday.'

'Here is a picture of you with your new bicycle,' I pointed out among the photos on the table.

'Yes, that's me.'

'You told me at one point, Ruth, that you went to the country in Sweden for the summers. Sweden must have been very important to you.'

'Yes, I may sometimes forget how important it was. I recovered my health; and people were very kind. I went to the country for three summers while there.

But my mother felt very bad, being supported, living on charity. 'I can't take this much longer,' she kept saying. 'I grew up giving charity, not taking charity.'

But everybody insisted: 'Why are you so upset about this, Pola? They seem to be nice about it.'

It wasn't that it was just the meager existence. It was very hard on my mother. She kept saying: 'I have to find work.'

One day she saw an ad in a Swedish newspaper. The Swedish Postal Banking System was looking for employees. She went. There were about a hundred people on line, she said, maybe more. And she stood on line.

Then it was time for her to go in. The gentleman talking and looking at her across the table, asked: 'Why should I hire you? Your Swedish is not very good.'

'Well, I speak English and I speak German,' she answered him. 'But the reason why you should hire me, is, that I'm very familiar with all modern electric office equipment.'

He thought this was hysterical from the little lady. My mother is actually shorter than me,' Ruth said laughing.

'That was because of her electrical supply store in Kozienice, right?'

'Yes, but she didn't have enough Swedish to explain it. But what was smart enough, was, that she switched into German, and he seemed to be impressed with her knowledge of that language. Then she switched into English. She realized that she was really on solid ground, because she spoke better English than him.

She was taking English classes at that point. She was bartering with another Jewish lady in our house. My mother was doing alterations for her. Do you remember?'

'Yes, I do. And didn't she also give lessons to you and Sarah?'

'Yes, the more work my mother could do for her – because she was an English teacher.

Now, the gentleman from the Postal Banking System said something, and an adding machine was brought in and a long list of numbers – an electric adding machine. My mother made herself comfortable and she was going on like this.' Ruth demonstrated how her mother magically worked with the numbers, adding them up with ease.

'You have the position,' he declared, obviously even more impressed.

You can't imagine what this did to my mother. We didn't move out. We were comfortable there. My mother paid her own way. She suddenly became a different person. It was as if she had grown a foot taller,' Ruth said smiling.

'She would hold up her head erect. She was paying her way. Although she had a long commute. She had a long walk to the bus stop on a dirt road. She waited for the bus in any kind of weather. The bus ride was about forty minutes.

In the village, which was almost deserted come wintertime, we realized that there were only three family homes on that road the year round. The other houses were just summer cottages, because they were near the lake.

My mother always came home from work with something she bought in the store for Sarah and me, usually something edible. She wasn't buying luxuries. But life now was very much better.

One day she came home and she brought bread, a freshly baked rye bread. 'This is called *tyska* bread,' she told everybody. 'You found Jewish bread!' they cried. 'Where did you find that bread?'

'There is a store not far from my work. They sell products to the German population. *Tyska* means German in Swedish,' she explained.

All the women wanted her to buy rye bread for them. 'I can't buy for each of you a whole rye bread,' she said. 'But I can share with you what I have.'

****

I remember a Sunday afternoon in Hödingen. It was after the war. We still were staying with the same farmer in the Russian zone. Food was scarce.

My two brothers and I were sitting at the kitchen table watching our mother cut a plum cake to share between us. The farmer's grandmother had secretly given my mother some plums so she could bake a cake. During the previous days she had taken off the cream from the milk she got on food stamps in the village shop.

We children could hardly wait for the moment when our mother would put a piece of cake and a spoonful of cream on each of our plates. Immediately we dug our fork into the plum cake she had baked the day before at the village bakery, like the other refugee women were doing.

I jealously eyed my brother's portions. They always got the biggest pieces, because I was the youngest, my mother would say. But I forgot my envy tasting the first bite of that deliciously juicy plum cake.

Hardly had we started when there was a knock at the door and the handle was pushed down at once. It was *Frau* Hoffmann, another refugee, who lived across the hall with her son. Luckily our mother had locked the door so we wouldn't need to share our delicacy with anyone. We children smiled at our mother for not allowing anyone to share our plum cake.

Frau Hoffmann must have known when we would sit down to eat, because on those occasions it was absolutely quiet in our kitchen. The extra food our mother could get hold of we ate in an almost holy silence.

****

'Now life was different,' Ruth reflected. 'Ruczka sent money to register Sarah in art school. Sarah went to art school a couple of times a week.

Then my cousin eventually worked it out with her new husband and she came. She was going to officially adopt Sarah in Sweden and take her back.'

'That must have been hard for you and your mom.'

'It was hard and it was good. I remembered Ruczka from the summers. To see her and hug Sarah! Ruczka brought us a lot of clothes. It was all secondhand clothes. Some were hers. Some were from her friends, and some from people she worked with. She had asked them, whether they had any outgrown children's clothes. She came with suitcases full. Things that didn't fit us we could be generous to hand out.

She arrived in Sweden and stayed with us. She didn't put on airs. She spent the first night in a hotel. Then she came with all her things and distributed it and stayed with us.

There was one room where there was a young woman named Adela. Sarah was sharing with her, so my mother could share with me. We didn't have three people sleep in a bed. Adela was from Czestochowa. Her family had had a bakery there. She was the only one to survive. But she had an aunt, her mother's sister, I believe, who lived in America. Her aunt had maybe rented the room.

That aunt was amazing. A neighbor's son, living in New York, in the Bronx, was in the military and was stationed in northern Germany at that point. She persuaded the mother to persuade her son to take a leave in Sweden to go and visit her niece in Germany.'

'And bring her back home?'

'Fell in love with her, married her and brought her home! Later they had three children.

Anyway, Sarah would move back in with us so that Ruczka could stay with Adela. It took weeks and weeks, or maybe even months to do all the paper work for the adoption. And then they left. That was done because Sarah needed an education.'

'She also needed parents. But, she had your mom.'

'She had my mom. Sarah hated to leave, because my mom was all she knew. She knew Ruczka because she lived in Warsaw, and Ruczka also lived in Warsaw. They had been running into each other.'

'Ruczka also came to your grandmother's house in the summer, right?'

'Every summer when she was younger, but not the last two summers.

Actually, Sarah was leaving with a stranger. My mother had been everything to her for six years. And then suddenly being kind of torn away, that was hard.'

'It must have been very hard.'

'But my mother already had a suspicion that it would take us long to come to the United States. My X-rays weren't coming up so good.'

'Was that about a year after you had been in Sweden?'

'Two years. And then Sarah left.

I mean, Ruczka just did wonderful things. She got a tutor for Sarah. They had a tutor for George too. George, her new husband's son, was already living with them in New York. Jurek was his name in Polish. He was trying to get into Rutgers University, any university.'

'Now, let's go back to you, Ruth. For how long did you stay in Sweden?'

'Two and a half years more. My mother was quite satisfied. She was working. She was self-supporting. There were still a lot of people leaving. Maryla and her aunt left for Australia. There were other people coming in. Life was OK. I was comfortable. My eleventh birthday was already after Sarah had left. I lost a cousin but I gained a bicycle.

And then the summers – it was customary that working or single mothers could send their children to the country. It was arranged by the authorities, whether by the local authorities, I don't know. The governmental authorities were running it.

My first stay in the country was with a schoolteacher. She had a cottage up on the hill and she was willing for the summer to take a fresh-air child.'

'That's what you were called?'

'Yes, a fresh-air child. I stayed with her. Sometimes we slept on the screened-in porch. We used kerosene lamps, and there was an outhouse. It was on the top of a hill. In the evening it was beautiful.

She had many friends; and on weekends they would come and they'd be dancing on the terrace and there would be a big *smorgasbord,* which means a table with mostly sandwiches.

She taught me how to wash my hair in rainwater. We had to carry water from the valley, water that was for drinking and cooking. There was a barrel of rainwater, and you took that for washing. It was rustic and lovely. We went down the hill to get our provisions. It was nice.

After that I stayed on a farm that was also very good. It was the summer of 1948, my second stay in the country. They had a bunch of us. A bunch of us were staying on that farm. Some of us had to help with milking the cows.

11th birthday of Ruth in Sweden (second from left) 1948

Later in America I impressed my children when we went to Sturbridge Village. That's in Massachusetts. It's a restored American village. As the farmer talked about how people used to milk the old ways, my kids popped up: 'Our mommy knows how to milk a cow!'

He was talking to a big group of American tourists. 'Well, would you mind showing us?' he asked me.

'Manually or with the machine?' I asked. I was taught to do both. The farmer I stayed with had one machine, but it was too slow to milk all the cows by pick-up time. That's why we had to milk some by hand.

Well, it came in handy. Everybody was in total awe. And I kept saying: 'I'm not in practice. It's been twenty years.' Ruth and I both had a good laugh.

'You knew all that from the farm, of course.'

'Yes, because we did chores. After milking the cows, we all went back into the house to this enormous farm breakfast. We were a group of ten or maybe twelve, a substantial group.

Their kids had all grown up, and it was hard to keep a farm going with just two older people. They weren't really old. They were middle-aged people. They treated us as if we were part of the family. What an enormous difference from the treatment in the camps,' Ruth exclaimed.

'We actually slept in another house nearby together with a schoolteacher. Later in the summer, when the hay had to be brought in, we were baling hay and we were bringing baskets of food out to the field. That was the third summer.

The places I stayed in were all different. But somehow the last summer with *tant* Frida was the most influential. But of course, the first summer I was just with my mother and in the hospital. That accounts for all four summers.

Tant Frida, I called her *tant* Frida. *Tant* means aunt.' Ruth showed me a picture of her and *tant* Frida.

'We went around everywhere on our bicycles. She needed company, because she was nursing her husband who had been paralyzed for a while from a stroke. He was a wonderful man. He was keeping himself occupied with stamps. People came with their stamp collections. He was quiet and calm. He had been a pianist all his life. *Tant* Frida had been an artist model.

They lived way off in Sweden near the Norwegian border in the town of Mora. It was far away from any big city. The husband told me that he had been a pianist for the silent movies. His playing had to set the mood of the movie. It was an exciting job that called for an accomplished pianist.

I had this quiet, calm man sitting in his room,' Ruth ruminated. 'I could use his desk, and he was sitting in a wheelchair. It was a nice sunny room that obviously had been the sitting room. I slept with *tant* Frida in the bedroom. The dining room was the dining room, and she served very formally.

I acquired very good table manners.' Ruth laughed.

'And she took me to all her friends. She also took me to the local museum, the Zorn Museum. The famous Swedish painter Anders Zorn had lived in Mora.

'The museum containing many of his works had been built next to the house he was born in,' *tant* Frida told me. As I was looking around, pointing at one of the paintings, I asked her: 'Doesn't she look like you?'

'That was me, when I was young,' she said smiling. She was now in her late 50s or early 60s. She actually appeared in many of his paintings.

You can understand how different that was from my former life,' Ruth said. 'I got to meet so many of her friends. One of her friends was also retired by this point. She was a widow. Her husband had been a Swedish sea captain.

She needed something to do. She took up photography and she became a photographer to one of the Swedish princesses, the crown princess. She gave me a necklace the princess had given her when she retired.'

'Is it the one you're wearing?'

'No. It's some kind of precious stone. I'll make sure to find it. It was sort of elaborate. I always kept it because it was a memento.

'I have no daughters,' she said to me. 'My nieces are all going to fight over it. And I like you better than them.'

This friend liked hiking. *Tant* Frida was not quite as limber and she didn't want to leave her paralyzed husband alone for too long. Sometimes we went on overnight hikes in the woods. She had a cabin where we could sleep over.

I did all the outdoor things, and she set me up with a knapsack. We did things I'd never done before. Unfortunately, I never got a chance to do them again until very much later in my life.

Those were very precious memories to me, very precious,' Ruth said nostalgically.

'Even though I had other summer moms. They were perfectly lovely people. But somehow during that summer with the Klarkqvists everything came together – the photographer and the art studio and all these things.

And the fact that it was a small town and everybody knew *tant* Frida well. We biked, people would stop and ask, and she then introduced me. I became this big spiel, you know what I am saying.

One day we were biking and I called out: 'I got to stop!' I had recognized a woman who was limping. She was a young Jewish woman who survived the Holocaust. I had met her in Stockholm. She was actually living in Stockholm with another Jewish woman who became quite a famous sculptor. They both stayed together.

She had lost a leg. She was brought on one of those transports of Jewish women. Some of the Swedish diplomats were pretty good at trying to get a few people out from the camps. She had come, and they fit her with a prosthesis. I recognized her.

We stopped and I introduced her to *tant* Frida. 'What are you doing here?' *tant* Frida asked her. 'Well, I want to see the country,' she replied. 'I am not working now.'

She was finishing her education. That was sponsored. The hundred women who were brought . . . they must have been sponsored by the Swedish government, I assume. I don't know exactly.

I met her, and *tant* Frida invited her spontaneously to share dinner with us and to meet her husband. It was just extremely special.'

'Did these women ever ask you about your experiences in the camps?' I asked Ruth. 'Did they ever wonder how difficult and life threatening your time was in the war?'

'It was tacitly agreed that we children should not be reminded of the horrors of the war,' Ruth explained. 'They believed that it would be easier to recover this way.'

Was Ruth already withdrawing from her war experiences, I wondered, and later, on coming to the United States did she purposely distance herself from them?

I remembered in fact, that she had decided, once she immigrated to the United States, to close all doors behind her about her camp and ghetto experiences.

But later in her life, after the early death of her cousin Sarah, the illness of her mother that caused her to forget the past, and the death of her husband Oscar, Ruth must have felt alone with her personal history. She probably regretted most of all not to have obtained more from her mother's memory reservoir.

'My mother realized that the problem with my lungs was not going to disappear,' Ruth continued at our next interview. 'No matter how pudgy I got, how healthy I was, no matter how many long hikes I had been able to take.

She decided to go back to the children's hospital, because when I had been there, there was a Jewish woman pediatrician who escaped from Poland. She couldn't work as a doctor but she could work as a doctor's assistant. She had been a pediatrician in Warsaw before the war.

My mother thought that this doctor needed to see me. And my mother needed to see her, to talk to her heart to heart.

The pediatrician explained to her: 'Look, it's scar tissue. Scar tissue will never go away. People will know when they look at it.' 'Do you know she has scar tissue?' my mother wanted to know. 'She doesn't test for TB. If she ever had TB it would show up on the test. Your daughter probably had pleurisy. It's an inflammation of the lining of the lungs.'

The pediatrician felt that my mom was hitting her head against the wall. 'Go somewhere else,' she suggested.

The only places I have a living family member is in New York and Buenos Aires, my mom pondered. Buenos Aires does not take Jews – only Germans.

My father's sister was trying to bring us there. They were willing to put up a bond. They had a wallpaper and paint store. Argentina wasn't taking any Jews. Aunt Sarah was sending us clothes. My mother didn't know what to do. Australia was taking Jews, gladly. 'But I don't know anybody in Australia and it's far, very far away,' my mom said.

It's not clear whether this woman suggested Canada, or my mother thought long enough and thought of Canada.'

'Which is not far away from America.'

'That's just it. It was probably my mother, but maybe the doctor mentioned the list of countries that didn't require X-rays. I have the feeling my mother asked:

'What countries don't require X-rays?' 'And she would know.'

****

After six years in Hödingen – before the Russian zone of Germany became the former GDR – my mother wanted to leave the East and go back to the West, to Hamburg. It was in the fall of 1949, the same year Ruth and her mother would leave Canada for the United States.

My mother had tried to flee with us once before, but we got caught. We were put into prison for a night, and the fifty West mark, my mother had saved from smuggling people over the border, was taken away from her.

A relative of my mother's friends, the Funkes, helped us finally in September 1949 to cross the border into the West. It was two weeks after we had been caught.

We were hiding our few belongings in a potato bag in a handcart under some brushwood. And with my dog we all left Hödingen in the direction of Walbeck, where this relative owned a field directly at the border. We were supposedly gathering berries and brushwood.

When we came to his field we saw Russian soldiers patrolling along the border. 'What are you doing here?' they wanted to know.

Our companion showed them a paper proving that the field belonged to him. 'This is my wife and these are my children. We are gathering berries and brushwood,' he explained.

The Russian soldiers checked his paper and then let us go. When they were out of sight he told us to run.

'And good luck!'

He filled up his handcart with plenty of brushwood and returned to the village.

On the other side of the border our dog suddenly smelled out a trace of a hare. He started barking as if he had gone crazy. But at this moment, I believe, we only thought about ourselves; about our newly won freedom, not about our savior who was, of course, still in danger, particularly because of our dog barking.

*****

11

Canada and New York

'Then came Canada. Suddenly my mother was fixated on Canada. She was racking her brain about who from Kozienice migrated to Canada. Kozienice had its episodes of anti-Semitism, as I told you, but it was not like Russia where people ran away from pogroms and poverty.

In Kozienice, if there was a family of ten children and things were very hard, the oldest son might be sent away to a place where jobs were plentiful. And Jews were permitted in. And he could send money back to the family.

My mom was racking her brain and she came up with two names of families whose sons had left for Canada. Not knowing their first name or other details, Pola Luksenburg wrote a letter to the Jewish community of Montreal. Just like that,' Ruth said proudly.

'Before the war two young men had left our town for Canada,' she wrote. 'Either of them could possibly be living in your vicinity.' She knew somehow that Montreal was the largest Jewish community in Canada. And lo and behold a few weeks later my mother got a letter back from a gentleman who remembered having played soccer with her brother. 'I played soccer with Daniel Luksenburg.'

That was luck.'

'That's your mother's brother who lived in Przemysl.'

'Yes, he was four kids away from my mother. As a married man Daniel lived in Przemysl. Visiting him is how my mother met my father.

Well, my mom knew somebody in Canada. She wrote him a long personal letter in Yiddish and told him our whole story. He was the principal of a Hebrew high school, who had grown children or growing children. He would sponsor us to immigrate, so we could become legal residents of Canada.

So off to Canada! From there it wasn't very far to the United States. And I didn't have to undergo a medical examination. We were very relieved.

Finally, our hope was rekindled to get to the United States to join Ruczka and Sarah. The aspect of joining them made us forget the years in

Sweden. We considered Canada one more necessary step on our odyssey from Poland to our final destination.

The gentleman sent papers from Montreal. My mom did all the paperwork. And we were off to Canada. He met us at the boat and took us to Montreal. He found us a place to stay with a poor Orthodox family, the Yagmans.

I finally remember their name. They raised a slew of children. Only the youngest daughter was still home. The husband was almost never home. He was a peddler. He still had the old-fashioned trade.

Mr. Yagman went, not with a wagon, but with a truck to the countryside, to small settlements. He was selling dish towels, bed linen, housewares, and so forth. He would come back on Friday and he would leave again on Sunday evening.

Mrs. Yagman was alone with that youngest of her children. She had plenty of space to spare a bedroom. We rented there. The gentleman who was helping us vouched that my mother came from a very Orthodox family, and she was extremely familiar with Jewish dietary laws, and would not confuse any of her utensils to be used.

If you are not familiar with these laws it could be very confusing,' Ruth told me.

'That's where we were going to live. In the poorest part of Montreal, in Rue Henri Julien, in the French speaking part of Montreal, in a run-down, inner-city neighborhood,' Ruth explained.

'The Yagmans were one of the few Orthodox families left. They spoke Yiddish, otherwise I would have been completely lost. Mrs. Yagman gave me instructions not to get into trouble in the street. 'Don't ever walk slowly. Walk to school briskly,' she said.

My mom got some kind of work. 'Nothing great,' as she said: 'but it's work.' She found a job in a factory making coats. She got me a coat, which was helpful.'

'Now you had to learn French.'

'You got it. That was my next crisis. I had to register. I was in the sixth grade now. I had to go to school. I couldn't just sit it out. The French-Canadian school taught one hour of English a day as a second language.

I was fine in English by this point, because in Sweden in the third grade you could pick a foreign language. The choice had been English or German. I knew enough German. I was learning grammatical English. I had third, fourth, and fifth grade English.

I knew we weren't going to stay in Canada. Nevertheless, I needed to know what the teacher was explaining to get through school. What was she saying? I needed a running translation.

I was going to use the techniques I had learned during the war: techniques of desperation, such as how can I find someone who speaks my language, or where can I hide? It was hell. I felt I was a drowning child.

Sarah was already in college in New York. And I, in the sixth grade, was trying to figure out what was going on. I was just searching for any lifeline in the class. I was desperate. Also, my mother was miserable at what she was doing. Luckily, she earned enough money to pay for a room and food.

I was sitting in class, thinking: I am starting all over again from the beginning. What am I going to do here? I was looking around. I needed to find someone who spoke my language. I didn't know any of the kids.

There were three boys who were wearing a *yarmulke*. That meant they were religious. But they were not ultra-religious because they would not be in a public school, where there are boys and girls together. They were not from extremely religious families. They were obviously poor because they lived in this neighborhood.

I thought I could try to approach one of them in Yiddish. It was likely that he knew Yiddish. I was doing all this plotting. The teacher was writing numbers on the blackboard, and I bent over to the back of the boy nearest me, who was wearing a *yarmulke*.

'Do you think you could translate for me into Yiddish whatever she says?' I asked him in Yiddish. 'Yeah,' sort of in a broad way, 'but what's in it for me?' he asked.

You know, if you get caught talking in class, you're going to be punished. I looked at the blackboard again, and everything looked familiar.

'You see this long division?' I suddenly asked him. 'I learned that in Sweden last year. What's in it for you,' I told him, 'are the answers to all the math problems.'

'That's a deal,' he whispered.

We both had a good chuckle. That's how I got through sixth grade,' Ruth said half laughing.

'You surely were resourceful.'

'My war techniques definitely helped. You become resourceful when you have to. Not everybody does, because – if you don't, you'll lose.

I still remember that I went to a Jewish school in Montreal, to a Workmen's Circle school. We were taught how to read and write Yiddish.

Until then I only knew how to talk Yiddish with my grandparents, and with all the women in the barracks.

After school was over at 3 p.m., I went home, picked up my Yiddish schoolbooks, and ran over to the Workmen's Circle school, which was only a short walk away from where we lived.

I can't tell you much more about my time in Canada. The only good thing was that Ruczka came to visit. She came once and brought clothes for us.

I probably suppressed most of what I experienced. It's just a period in my life I don't care to remember, I guess. It was just a step to our ultimate goal, which was to reunite with Ruczka and Sarah.

After about a year my mother decided to apply for immigration at the American embassy, which we did. It was fairly quick from Canada, since we were now legal residents of Canada. It was after about a year and a half that we left.

The Canadian authorities gave us papers to immigrate, which would let my mother and me cross the border into the United States,' Ruth explained.

'We got on the train in Montreal. It stopped in upstate New York in a small village called Rouses Point. Canadian police stepped off. American immigration came on the train, checked everybody's documents. Our documents were fine.

And when our train finally pulled into New York's Grand Central Station we saw Ruczka, standing on the platform waving to us.'

I would like to thank the Ravina family and Joseph Charles Teutsch and his wife Nicole Farnsworth for their generous subvention.